D0547742

bake it

MURDOCH BOOKS

contents

baking

Although the word 'baking' can define, in its most general sense, a whole range of items cooked in an oven, it primarily refers to flour-based goods such as breads, cakes and pastries. Baked goods have evolved from a very basic flat 'cake' cooked on a griddle without the aid of any leaveners, to those that were made after the discovery of yeast fermentation. This in turn brought about breads, then, as people developed greater skills and discovered new ingredients, such as baking powder, other baked goods such as cakes began to appear. From this, biscuits evolved and, finally, more specialized and elaborate pies and pastries.

For centuries, people have been turning flour into food with the help of little more than water. Today, baking remains a pleasure and a passion for many of us who have fallen in love with this fascinating and age-old tradition.

basic equipment

To bake well, you will need to invest in a few basic pieces of equipment. Not all are essential — start with a few items of good-quality bakeware and slowly build up your collection.

weighing scales: Electronic scales are the most accurate. Balance scales work equally well, but must be able to be accurate to as little as 5 g (1/8 oz).

measuring cups and spoons: If using cup measures, you will need 1/4, 1/3, 1/2 and 1 cup sizes. A measuring jug (pitcher) is essential for measuring liquids. Measuring spoons come as a set: 1 tablespoon (20 ml), 1 teaspoon (5 ml), 1/2 teaspoon and 1/4 teaspoon. All dry ingredients should be levelled off with a knife when measuring ingredients using cups or spoons.

mixing bowls: It is useful to have a set each of glass and metal mixing bowls. Stainless steel bowls are durable and good conductors of heat and cold. Heatproof bowls are essential for slow heating over a water bath.

mixers: Hand-held electric mixers are essential for cake-making and are relatively inexpensive. An electric stand mixer, with its many attachments, can be used for kneading bread dough, whisking egg whites and creaming cake and biscuit doughs. A stand mixer is an expensive item and although not essential, most serious home bakers find them a good investment. Food processors are great for making pastry dough and some biscuit doughs.

whisks: A balloon whisk is useful for whisking egg whites, smaller quantities of cream, and more delicate fillings that can easily be overwhisked using an electric mixer. Small and large sizes are available.

spoons: Wooden spoons are used for beating and mixing and do not conduct heat or scratch non-stick surfaces. Large metal spoons are best for folding in dry ingredients, as their sharp edges cut easily through the mixture without losing too much air.

spatulas: Used to scrape a bowl completely clean. Rubber spatulas are more flexible than plastic ones but tend to absorb colour and flavour, so keep separate ones for sweet and savoury use.

palette knives: A knife with a thin, flat blade with a rounded end. Useful for transferring flat items such as biscuits from the tray to the cooling rack, and for spreading icings.

rolling pins: A long wooden rolling pin, about 48 cm (19 inches) long and 4 cm (1 1/2 inches) in diameter, is the best all-round pin. Wood is preferable to ceramic or marble as its surface collects and holds a fine layer of flour.

sieves: Larger sieves are essential for sifting flour, while a small one is useful for sprinkling icing (confectioners') sugar or cocoa powder over baked goods. (Dredgers, similar in appearance to a salt shaker, may also be used to do this.) Buy a sieve that has a lip so it can rest on the edge of the bowl.

pastry brushes and wheels: You will need a pastry brush for glazing bread and pastry doughs, as well as sealing pastry pie dough. Take care when using a brush with nylon bristles with hot liquids as the bristles may melt. Metal or plastic pastry wheels are used for cutting fluted edges on pastry.

oven thermometers: Designed to stand or hang in the oven. When doing any baking, it is essential to check that the temperature is accurate. The 'calibration' of in-built oven thermometers can slip in accuracy over time.

baking trays: The best are the flat sheets with either one or both ends turned. The flat sides mean you can easily slide things off. Buy heavy trays that heat evenly and don't warp. If making biscuits you will need two trays.

baking tins: Breads, cakes, pastries and puddings all need different shapes and sizes of tins. Use the tin specified where possible, as using a different capacity tin will affect cooking times. Always buy good-quality bakeware.

speciality tins: When baking, a few speciality tins are required — loaf tins for bread, as well as spring-form tins, kugelhopf, muffin and friand tins, to name a few (see pages 15–17).

cake testers: These are long, thin, purpose-built skewers with a sharp pointed edge, used for testing to see whether a cake is cooked.

cooling racks: These may be round, square or rectangular. The metal grids enable air to circulate around the food during cooling.

mixing bowls

Buy a selection of glass and metal mixing bowls. Heatproof bowls are essential for heating over a water bath.

measuring cups & spoons

All dry ingredients should be levelled off with a knife when using measuring cups or spoons.

whisks

Balloon whisks range from large ones for whisking egg whites to smaller ones used for batters and sauces.

spatulas

Used for scraping a bowl completely clean. Rubber spatulas are more flexible than plastic ones.

rolling pins

These should be large enough to roll out a full sheet of pastry. Good-quality rolling pins are made from hard wood and have a very smooth finish.

sieves & dredgers

Sieves are used to sift flour or to dust flour onto the work surface. Use a small sieve or a dredger when dusting baked goods with icing (confectioners') sugar or cocoa powder.

pastry wheel

Used for cutting fluted edges on pastry.

pastry brushes

Used for glazing bread and pastry doughs, as well as sealing pastry pie dough.

shallow tins

Used for baking slices (bars) and brownies. A Swiss (jelly) roll tin is used for baking the sponge needed for roulades and Swiss rolls.

baking trays

Buy heavy trays that heat evenly and don't warp. If making biscuits you will need two trays.

round & square tins

Breads, cakes, biscuits and pastries all require different tins of varying shapes and sizes. Use the tin specified where possible, as using a different capacity tin will affect cooking times.

loaf tins

Used for baking breads and pound cakes.

Buy tins with welded, non-leaking seams.

spring-form tins

Used for baking cakes such as cheesecakes or fragile cakes,
as the spring clip can be unbuckled and the side of the tin gently
eased away from the cake.

tartlet tins

These fluted tartlet tins have a loose base so you can easily
remove the tart. Large tins, in various sizes and depths, are
also available, with or without fluted edges.

kugelhopf tins

A fluted tin with a rounded base and a funnel down the centre. Available in large and small sizes and various patterns.

friand tins

Sold either as individual tins or as a 12-hole tin, sometimes with patterns on the base.

breads and muffins

about breads

Bread-making can be traced back almost 8000 years to the fertile plains of Iran, Iraq, Syria and Egypt. Riverside dwellers made a thick, gruel-like porridge from soaked grain, which they made into a flat cake and cooked on heated stones. However, they discovered that if left exposed to the air, tiny natural yeast particles would sour the porridge as fermentation took place. When it was cooked, the resulting 'cake' had a lighter texture and a pleasant tangy flavour — this was the first recorded bread. The ancient Egyptians developed purpose-built ovens, and were the first people to employ professional bakers. Wheat was relatively scarce so bread was usually made with other types of flour, such as rye and barley, which produced a dark, dense bread. Later, the Romans began large-scale milling, producing finer flours. They also set up professional guilds to teach the trade. From here the process was introduced into Europe and, for centuries, methods changed very little.

breads today

Today breads are flavoured in many different ways, made with various types of flour, and baked either in tins to give them definite shapes, or freeform. While white bread was once the bread of the upper classes and regarded as infinitely superior (wholegrain breads were considered to be the bread of peasants), these days the reverse is often true, and dense, wholegrain breads are back in style.

We make breads using commercial yeast (either fresh or dried) or with chemical raising agents such as baking powder. Yeast is used to leaven a wide range of different breads, from a basic loaf to pizza bases. The dough may be enriched with eggs and butter, sweetened with sugar and honey and enhanced with chocolate, spices, herbs, nuts, seeds and cheese, to name a few.

Then there are quick breads, such as muffins and scones, which require very little preparation time. Made using a chemical raising agent, such as baking powder or bicarbonate of soda (baking soda), rather than yeast to leaven them, quick breads are baked as soon as they've been mixed. They don't need to be left to rise and are ready in no time at all. Quick breads come in various forms; firm doughs are shaped, while softer doughs can be rolled and stamped into scones. Softer batters are poured into a tin and baked, while cake-like mixtures such as muffins can be cooked in individual moulds. Quick breads, both sweet and savoury, can be flavoured and enriched in much the same way as yeast breads.

Throughout the culinary world, bread is a symbol of sustenance, and is eaten at all times of the day. There is nothing better than good bread fresh from the oven, with its heady aroma, crisp golden crust and soft, light crumb. Whether we slather bread with butter while it is still warm, sandwich it or use it to mop up a stew or soup, bread is undeniably a part of our everyday life.

essential ingredients

Flour supplies structure to bread, leaveners aerate the dough and give it a specific texture, salt balances the flavours and helps control the aeration of yeast breads, and liquid binds everything together. Other ingredients are added to enrich the dough and enhance its flavour and texture.

wheat flour

Wheat provides the main source of flour used in bread-making. It has a higher protein content than other flours, which makes it the most suitable flour for yeast breads. The wheat grain is made up of three parts: the bran (husk), the germ and endosperm. Different types of flour contain varying percentages of one or all of these.

white bread (strong) flour: Milled from the endosperm, which has a high protein content. When the proteins come into contact with liquid during kneading, they produce gluten, an elastic web of strands that traps the carbon dioxide gases given off by yeast fermentation. These gases allow the bread to rise. Bread flour is available from large supermarkets or health-food stores. If unavailable, substitute with unbleached plain (all-purpose) flour.

plain (all-purpose) flour: Used in quick breads when either baking powder or bicarbonate of soda (baking soda) is used to leaven the dough. It contains less gluten than bread flour.

self-raising flour: This is plain flour with baking powder and salt already added. It is suitable only for use in quick breads.

wholemeal (whole-wheat) flour: Made from the whole grain. It gives a nutty flavour and dense texture to bread. Often used with white bread flour.

semolina: Made from the endosperm of durum wheat. Used in combination with white bread flour. Adds texture and flavour to breads.

bran (husk): The hard fibrous outer coating of the wheat grain. Used in some quick breads, such as muffins, to add texture.

other flours

All other flours used in bread-making are used in combination with bread or plain flour, adding a unique flavour as well as texture to bread.

rye flour: This is popular in many Northern European and Scandinavian countries, where it is the major grain variety grown. It produces a dark, dense bread with a pleasant earthy flavour when combined with bread flour.

oatmeal: More coarsely ground than most grains. It is available fine, medium or course ground and adds texture as well as flavour to bread.

polenta (cornmeal): A coarse yellow grain ground from maize. It adds a wonderfully nutty flavour and crunchy texture to bread. It can be used on its own in quick breads, but is always used in combination with bread flour in yeast breads.

leaveners

Breads are leavened with yeast or a chemical raising agent. Yeast is a single-celled fungus that leavens bread by feeding on the natural sugars present in flour. Once it is mixed with flour and liquid, yeast produces carbon dioxide and alcohol — this process is known as fermentation. As the dough bakes, the carbon dioxide gases expand, giving bread its characteristic chewy texture, taste and lightness.

yeast: Available in three forms — fresh, active dried and instant dried. Both fresh yeast and active dried yeast need to be dissolved in liquid before they can be mixed with flour. Instant dried yeast is more versatile, as it can be added directly to the flour without needing to be dissolved first. Instant dried yeast is used in all the yeasted bread recipes in this book.

baking powder and bicarbonate of soda (baking soda): These are the two chemical leavening agents used to make quick breads. As soon as they are mixed with a liquid they start producing carbon dioxide, and the dough must be baked at once so that the precious gases are not lost, or the dough will not rise. Baking powder is a mixture of bicarbonate of soda and cream of tartar. Bicarbonate of soda needs an acid, such as cream of tartar, buttermilk, yoghurt, sour cream, or vinegar or lemon juice, to activate it.

salt

Salt is essential for flavour in bread. It also helps to tighten the elastic web of gluten strands (which traps the carbon dioxide gases given off by yeast fermentation), improving the volume of the finished loaf.

liquid

water: Used in breads to bind the ingredients and add moisture. In yeast breads, the water is warmed first as the warmth stimulates the yeast into action. If the water is too cold, the yeast will not activate fully; too hot, and the yeast will be killed. The ideal temperature for water is 32–48°C (90–120°F). The water should be tepid or hand hot.

milk: Sometimes used in breads and, like water, is usually warmed first. Milk softens bread dough and adds a little extra colour to the crust.

buttermilk and yoghurt: These are sometimes used, giving the bread a delicate sour flavour.

optional additions

sweeteners: Sugar is often added to boost yeast activity, especially if the bread is made with a heavier flour such as wholemeal (whole-wheat) or rye. All types of sugar can be used, including honey, maple syrup and molasses.

fats: Fats such as butter or oil tenderize bread dough and give it a soft, golden crumb. Breads made with a high percentage of fat will have a more cake-like texture. Fats also slow down the action of the yeast, and dough enriched with a high proportion of butter and oil will take longer to rise.

eggs: These enrich bread dough and produce a lighter, more golden bread. Their water content adds moisture, while the fat content tenderizes the dough, giving a softer crumb.

other ingredients: Nuts, dried fruits, chocolate, olives, herbs, spices, cheese and vegetables are just some of the many ingredients that may be added to breads to enhance their flavour.

making the dough

using dried yeast

Breads made using instant dried yeast can be made in two ways. The dried yeast may be combined with some of the warmed liquid and left to foam, or the yeast may be mixed directly in with the flour and then kneaded.

foaming the yeast: Sprinkle the dried yeast and sugar (if using) over the warmed liquid in a small bowl and stir to dissolve the sugar. Leave in a draught-free place for 10 minutes, or until the mixture develops a foam. If making bread using an electric mixer with a dough hook attachment (the dough hook makes easy work of the kneading process), put the flour and salt in the bowl of the mixer. Pour in the foamed yeast mixture and remaining liquid. With the mixer set to its lowest speed, mix the ingredients for about 2 minutes, or until a loose batter is formed (you can use either the paddle or dough hook attachment to do this). Increase the speed to medium and, using the dough hook, knead for 6–8 minutes, or until the dough is smooth, shiny and elastic (when a finger is pressed into the dough, it should spring back immediately).

Alternatively, if making the bread by hand, put the flour and salt in a large bowl and make a well. Pour in the foamed yeast (and sugar, if using) and remaining liquid and, using a wooden spoon, bring the ingredients together to form a sticky mass. Shape into a ball and transfer to a lightly floured surface. Knead the dough for 10 minutes, or until it is smooth and elastic. To knead the dough by hand, use the heel of your hand to push the dough from the centre of the ball away from you, and then turn the dough 45 degrees and draw it back into the centre. Repeat this process of turning and kneading until the dough is smooth, shiny and elastic.

stirring the yeast directly into the flour: Put the flour and salt into the bowl of an electric mixer, stir in the instant dried yeast and any sugar, and then pour in the warmed liquid. With the mixer set to its lowest speed, work the dough for 2 minutes, or until it comes together. Then, increase the speed to medium and continue to knead for 6–8 minutes, or until the dough is smooth, shiny and elastic. The dough can also be made by hand (as explained above).

leaving the dough to rise

Shape the dough into a ball and put it in a large, lightly oiled bowl, turning to coat the surface of the dough in the oil. Cover the bowl with plastic wrap and leave to rise in a draught-free place for 1–2 hours, or until the dough has doubled in size. Heavier or enriched doughs will take longer to rise.

Ambient room temperature is the perfect environment for the bread to rise, rather than in a room that is too hot — a slower, unforced rise gives a better flavoured bread. You can also allow bread to rise overnight in the refrigerator; the cold doesn't kill the yeast, it merely retards it. If leaving bread to rise in the refrigerator, remove and leave at room temperature for about 2 hours before shaping it.

knocking back

Knock back the dough by punching it gently (this will knock out the air to reduce the volume) and turn out onto a lightly floured surface. If making bread rolls or buns, use a knife to cut the dough into even-sized pieces. Using your hands, work the dough into the specified shape. The dough can be either pressed into a tin or placed on a lightly floured baking tray.

shaping and scoring

if baking in a tin: Lightly grease the inside of the specified tin with oil or butter. Shape the dough into an oval of roughly the same dimensions as the tin and, with the seam facing downwards, gently press into the tin. Cover the dough with a clean, lightly dampened cloth and leave to rise for a second time until the dough reaches the top of the tin, which may take 30–45 minutes.

if baking on a tray: Lightly grease and/or dust a baking tray with white bread (strong) flour (or as specified). Shape the prepared dough as specified in the recipe and transfer to the tray, placing the dough seam side down. Cover the dough with a lightly dampened cloth and leave to rise for a second time until the dough has doubled in size, which may take 30–45 minutes.

If the recipe specifies to score the dough, use a small sharp knife and cut gently but firmly down through the dough, without pulling or tearing it. These cuts are not only decorative but they also allow the bread to expand as it bakes.

glazing

Some recipes ask for the dough to be glazed. The glaze should be lightly brushed over the surface of the dough using a pastry brush. Avoid brushing the glaze onto the rim of the tin or the baking tray, as this can cause the dough to stick to the tin and tear as it rises.

Different glazes produce different effects. A glaze of egg yolks beaten with a little milk will give a shiny golden crust. Melted butter will result in a soft crust, and water will give the dough a crisp crust (spray the dough lightly with a water atomizer). Breads are sometimes dusted with flour to give them a rustic charm and a chewy crust.

hints and tips

yeast breads

- When adding water to yeast (or a yeast and flour mixture), warm it first until tepid or hand hot. Do not use water that is too hot to touch or it will kill the yeast.

- If dissolving yeast first, leave it in a warm place for at least 10 minutes, or until a good foam appears on the surface. If it does not foam, the yeast is dead and you will have to start again with a new batch.

- If mixing dough by hand use a wooden spoon to bring the ingredients together. The dough should feel sticky when it first comes together. If it feels dry, add a little more water, a tablespoon at a time.

- If using an electric stand mixer always use the dough attachment, unless otherwise specified. Stand the mixer well away from the edge of the work surface because it may move as it is mixing the dough.

- Always start with the electric mixer on its lowest setting to first mix the ingredients, then increase the speed to medium to knead the dough.

- When leaving dough to rise, use a large bowl at least twice the size of the dough so it has plenty of room to expand.

- Lightly oil both the bowl and the surface of the dough before leaving the dough to rise. The dough should be covered with plastic wrap to prevent it forming a skin, which prevents it rising properly.

- To test if a dough has risen sufficiently, press a finger into the surface. The fingerprint should remain indented and should not spring back.

- Draughts can cause dough to deflate, so make sure the room is draught-free. Doughs will rise too fast if the room is overly hot, which will give an unpleasant smell and flavour to the bread. If this happens, deflate the dough and leave to rise again in a cool place (for at least 1 hour to develop flavour).

- Lightly flour the work surface before shaping the dough.

- If leaving bread dough overnight in the refrigerator, allow time for it to return to room temperature so it can begin to rise. This should take 45–60 minutes.

- Always grease the tin with spray oil or melted butter. Baking trays should be lightly greased or dusted with flour.

- When pressing dough into a tin it should reach to 1.5 cm (1/2 inch) below the top of the tin. After rising, the centre of the dough should protrude about 2.5 cm (1 inch) above the top of the tin. The dough is then ready to be baked.

- Never open the oven door during the first half of the total baking time or the bread can collapse. If you do need to turn the bread to get even browning, do this after the halfway point.

- To test if a bread is cooked, gently remove it from the tray or tin and tap it on the bottom — it should sound hollow. If it doesn't, return it to the oven for a further 5 minutes, then test again.

- Store bread in a paper or cloth bag for up to 24 hours in a cool place. Do not refrigerate bread as this makes it become stale more quickly. If keeping bread longer, store in a plastic bag or a zip lock bag.

- To freeze bread, wrap it in plastic wrap and then place inside a freezer bag. Defrost to room temperature before use. Bread that is allowed to defrost slowly, at room temperature, will retain its freshness for longer.

quick breads

- Always weigh ingredients carefully and weigh everything first before you start mixing anything.

- Grease tins and line them with baking paper, if needed, before you start preparing the dough.

- Always bake quick breads as soon as possible after mixing.

simple white bread

makes one 25 cm (10 inch) oval loaf

2¹/2 teaspoons (7 g) **instant dried yeast**

1 teaspoon **caster (superfine) sugar**

450 g (1 lb/3²/3 cups) **white bread (strong) flour**

Sprinkle the yeast and sugar over 150 ml (5 fl oz) warm water in a small bowl. Stir to dissolve the sugar, then leave in a draught-free place for 10 minutes, or until the yeast is foamy.

Combine the flour and 2 teaspoons salt in the bowl of an electric mixer with a dough hook attachment and make a well in the centre. Add another 150 ml (5 fl oz) warm water to the yeast mixture, then pour the mixture into the well. With the mixer set to the lowest speed, mix for 2 minutes, or until a dough forms. Increase the speed to medium and knead the dough for another 10 minutes, or until it is smooth and elastic. Alternatively, mix the dough by hand using a wooden spoon, then turn out onto a floured work surface and knead the dough for 10 minutes, or until smooth and elastic.

Grease a large bowl with oil, then transfer the dough to the bowl, turning the dough to coat in the oil. Cover with plastic wrap and leave to rise in a draught-free place for 1–1¹/2 hours, or until the dough has doubled in size.

Knock back the dough by punching it gently, then turn out onto a lightly floured work surface. Shape into a rounded oval and transfer to a greased baking tray. Cover loosely with a damp cloth and leave for 30 minutes, or until doubled in size. Meanwhile, preheat the oven to 190°C (375°F/Gas 5).

Using a sharp knife, make three diagonal slashes, about 4 cm (1¹/2 inches) apart, on the top of the loaf. Bake the loaf for 40 minutes, or until it sounds hollow when tapped on the base. Transfer to a wire rack to cool completely.

tip Because home-baked bread has no preservatives, it is best eaten on the day of baking; otherwise, use it to make toast. Bread can also be tightly wrapped and frozen for up to 3 months.

finnish cardamom rings

makes 16

1 tablespoon (12 g) **instant dried yeast**

115 g (4 oz/1/2 cup) **caster (superfine) sugar**

200 ml (7 fl oz) **evaporated milk**

2 **eggs**, lightly beaten

80 g (23/4 oz/1/2 cup) **wholemeal (whole-wheat) flour**

500 g (1 lb 2 oz/4 cups) **white bread (strong) flour**

11/2 teaspoons **ground cardamom**

50 g (13/4 oz) **unsalted butter**, softened

glaze

1 **egg**

60 ml (2 fl oz/1/4 cup) **milk**

bake it

Sprinkle the **yeast** and sugar over the water and **leave** in a draught-free place until the yeast is foamy.

Add the remaining **flour** then, using the dough **hook**, knead until the dough is smooth and elastic.

Sprinkle the yeast and 1 teaspoon of the sugar over 125 ml (4 fl oz/1/2 cup) warm water in a small bowl. Stir to dissolve the sugar, then leave in a draught-free place for 10 minutes, or until the yeast is foamy.

Combine the evaporated milk and eggs in a small bowl and stir to mix well.

Combine the wholemeal flour, 250 g (9 oz/2 cups) of the white bread flour, the cardamom, remaining sugar and 1 1/2 teaspoons salt in the bowl of an electric mixer with a dough hook attachment and make a well in the centre. Pour in the yeast and evaporated milk mixtures. With the mixer set to the lowest speed, mix for 1 minute, or until a dough forms. Add the butter and mix to combine well. Add the remaining flour, 60 g (2 1/4 oz/1/2 cup) at a time, and knead for 10 minutes, or until the dough is smooth and elastic (the dough will be very soft).

Grease a large bowl with oil, then transfer the dough to the bowl, turning the dough to coat in the oil. Cover with plastic wrap and leave to rise in a draught-free place for 1–1 1/2 hours, or until the dough has doubled in size.

Knock back the dough by punching it gently, then turn out onto a floured work surface. Divide the dough into 16 equal portions. Using your hands, roll each piece of dough to measure 25 cm (10 inches) in length, then join the ends to form a ring. Gently press the joins to seal. Transfer the rings to two lightly greased baking trays. Cover loosely with a damp cloth and leave for 45 minutes, or until doubled in size. Meanwhile, preheat the oven to 180°C (350°F/Gas 4).

To make the glaze, whisk together the egg and milk and brush it over the rings. Bake for 18–20 minutes, or until golden.

italian dried fruit buns

makes 12

90 g (3¼ oz/¾ cup) **raisins**

3 teaspoons (9 g) **instant dried yeast**

80 g (2¾ oz/⅓ cup) **caster (superfine) sugar**

400 g (14 oz/3¼ cups) **white bread (strong) flour**

1 teaspoon **almond essence**

1 tablespoon **olive oil**

finely grated **zest** from 1 **orange**

40 g (1½ oz/¼ cup) **mixed peel**

40 g (1½ oz/¼ cup) **pine nuts**

1 **egg**, lightly beaten

115 g (4 oz/½ cup) **caster (superfine) sugar**, extra

Cover the raisins with 250 ml (9 fl oz/1 cup) boiling water in a small bowl and set aside for 20 minutes. Drain, reserving the liquid. Put half the liquid into a bowl, add the yeast, a pinch of the sugar and 30 g (1 oz/¼ cup) of the flour. Stir to combine, then leave in a draught-free place for 10 minutes, or until the yeast is foamy.

Sift the remaining flour, sugar and 1 teaspoon salt into the bowl of an electric mixer with a dough hook attachment and make a well in the centre. Combine the remaining raisin water with the almond essence and oil, then pour it, along with the yeast mixture, into the well. Add the raisins, orange zest, mixed peel and pine nuts. With the mixer set to the lowest speed, mix until a dough forms. Increase the speed to medium and knead the dough for 5 minutes, or until it is smooth and elastic; add a little more flour if necessary. Alternatively, mix the dough by hand using a wooden spoon, then turn out onto a floured work surface and knead for 5 minutes, or until smooth and elastic.

Grease a large bowl with oil, then transfer the dough to the bowl, turning the dough to coat in the oil. Cover with plastic wrap and leave to rise in a draught-free place for 2 hours, or until the dough has doubled in size.

Knock back the dough by punching it gently, then turn out onto a lightly floured work surface. Divide the dough into 12 equal portions and shape each piece into an oval. To glaze the rolls, coat them in egg, then roll them in the extra sugar to coat. Transfer the rolls to a greased baking tray and leave for 30–40 minutes, or until the rolls have risen a little (they won't quite double in size). Meanwhile, preheat the oven to 200°C (400°F/Gas 6).

Bake the rolls for 15 minutes, or until golden, then transfer to a wire rack to cool.

saffron currant bread

makes one 25 cm (10 inch) ring

110 g (3³/4 oz/³/4 cup) **currants**

2 tablespoons **dry sherry** or **rum**

60 ml (2 fl oz/1/4 cup) **milk**

1/4 teaspoon **saffron threads**

1 tablespoon (12 g) **instant dried yeast**

115 g (4 oz/1/2 cup) **caster (superfine) sugar**

125 g (41/2 oz) **unsalted butter**, softened

3 **eggs**

25 g (1 oz/1/4 cup) **ground almonds**

grated **zest** from 1 **orange**

375 g (13 oz/3 cups) **plain (all-purpose) flour**

icing (confectioners') sugar, for dusting

Combine the currants and sherry in a small bowl and set aside for 30 minutes. Heat the milk in a small saucepan over medium heat until the milk reaches simmering point, then remove from the heat. Add the saffron and set aside for 20 minutes to allow the saffron to infuse.

Sprinkle the yeast and a pinch of the sugar over 60 ml (2 fl oz/1/4 cup) warm water in a small bowl. Stir to dissolve the sugar, then leave in a draught-free place for 10 minutes, or until the yeast is foamy. Grease a 25 cm (10 inch) ring tin.

Cream the butter and remaining sugar in a bowl using an electric mixer until pale and fluffy. Add the eggs one at a time, beating well after each addition. Add 1/2 teaspoon salt, the milk and yeast mixtures, ground almonds, orange zest and currant mixture and beat gently to combine. Add the flour, 60 g (21/4 oz/1/2 cup) at a time, and mix until incorporated. Using the lowest speed, beat the mixture for another 5 minutes, or until the dough is shiny and elastic (the dough will be soft).

Spoon the dough into the prepared ring tin and cover with plastic wrap. Leave to rise in a draught-free place for 11/2–2 hours, or until the dough has doubled in size. Meanwhile, preheat the oven to 180°C (350°F/Gas 4).

Bake the bread for 35–40 minutes, or until golden, and a skewer inserted into the centre of the bread comes out clean. Cool in the tin for 10 minutes, then turn out onto a wire rack to cool. Serve dusted with icing sugar.

pumpernickel rolls

makes 12 lunch rolls or 16 dinner rolls

90 g (3¹/4 oz/¹/4 cup) **molasses**

30 g (1 oz) **butter**

1 tablespoon (12 g) **instant dried yeast**

30 g (1 oz/¹/4 cup) **unsweetened cocoa powder**

1 tablespoon **soft brown sugar**

1¹/2 tablespoons **caraway seeds**

2 teaspoons **fennel seeds**

300 g (10¹/2 oz/3 cups) **rye flour**, plus extra for dusting

375 g (13 oz/3 cups) **white bread (strong) flour**

Mix **the ingredients** together until the dough is **smooth** and elastic.

Use a **floured knife** to make a cut across the tops of the **rolls**.

Heat 500 ml (17 fl oz/2 cups) water, the molasses and butter in a small saucepan over low heat until the butter has melted.

Combine the yeast, cocoa powder, sugar, caraway seeds, fennel seeds, 200 g (7 oz/2 cups) of rye flour and 1 teaspoon salt in the bowl of an electric mixer with a dough hook attachment. Pour in the butter mixture and, with the mixer set to the lowest speed, mix until the ingredients are incorporated, scraping down the bowl as necessary. Add the remaining rye flour and mix for 2 minutes. Add the bread flour, 60 g (2 1/4 oz/1/2 cup) at a time, mixing to form a soft dough. Increase the speed to medium and knead for 5 minutes, or until the dough is smooth and elastic. Alternatively, mix the dough by hand using a wooden spoon, then turn out onto a floured work surface and knead for 5 minutes, or until smooth and elastic.

Grease a large bowl with oil, then transfer the dough to the bowl, turning the dough to coat in the oil. Cover with plastic wrap and leave to rise in a draught-free place for 45–60 minutes, or until the dough has doubled in size.

Knock back the dough by punching it gently, then turn out onto a floured work surface and divide into 12 equal portions (or 16 if making dinner rolls). Shape each piece into a round, then gently roll to form an oval shape. Transfer the rolls to greased baking trays and dust the tops with extra rye flour. Using a sharp, lightly floured knife, make a 1 cm (1/2 inch) deep cut across the top of each roll. Cover with a damp cloth and leave for 45 minutes, or until doubled in size. Meanwhile, preheat the oven to 180°C (350°F/Gas 4).

Bake the rolls for 35 minutes (or 25–30 minutes for the dinner rolls), or until they sound hollow when tapped on the base. Transfer to a wire rack to cool. Serve the rolls with cheese, olives, smoked salmon and dill pickles.

tip When dividing the dough into portions, weigh each portion so they are all the same size.

currant cream scones

makes 12 scones

375 g (13 oz/3 cups) **plain (all-purpose) flour**

1 1/2 teaspoons **bicarbonate of soda (baking soda)**

3 teaspoons **cream of tartar**

1 teaspoon **mixed (pumpkin pie) spice**

2 teaspoons **caster (superfine) sugar**, plus extra for sprinkling

50 g (1 3/4 oz) **unsalted butter**, chilled and diced

150 ml (5 fl oz) **pouring cream**

150 ml (5 fl oz) **milk,** plus extra for brushing

125 g (4 1/2 oz/3/4 cup) **currants**

jam and **thick (double/heavy) cream,** to serve

Preheat the oven to 220°C (425°F/Gas 7). Grease a baking tray or line the tray with baking paper.

Sift the flour, bicarbonate of soda, cream of tartar, mixed spice and sugar into a large bowl. Using your fingertips, rub in the butter until the mixture resembles breadcrumbs. Add the cream, milk and currants and mix with a flat-bladed knife to form a soft dough, adding a little extra flour if the mixture is too sticky.

Using floured hands, gently gather the dough together and lift out onto a lightly floured work surface. Pat into a smooth ball, then press out to a 2 cm (3/4 inch) thickness. Using a 6 cm (2 1/2 inch) pastry cutter, cut the dough into rounds, or use a knife dipped in flour to cut 4 cm (1 1/2 inch) squares.

Place the scones on the baking tray, brush the tops lightly with milk and sprinkle with the extra sugar. Bake for 10–12 minutes, or until golden. Transfer to a wire rack lined with a tea towel (dish towel). Serve the scones warm with marmalade or jam and thick cream.

tip When making scones, handle the mixture with care. Don't be too heavy-handed when mixing the dough or the scones will be tough.

middle eastern lamb and pine nut pizzas

makes 6

1 1/2 teaspoons (4 1/2 g) **instant dried yeast**

1/2 teaspoon **caster (superfine) sugar**

450 g (1 lb/3 2/3 cups) **white bread (strong) flour**

1 tablespoon **olive oil**

lemon wedges, to serve

Greek-style yoghurt, to serve

topping

2 tablespoons **olive oil**

1 small **onion**, finely chopped

1 **garlic clove**, finely chopped

250 g (9 oz) **minced (ground) lamb**

400 g (14 oz) **tinned tomatoes**, drained and chopped

40 g (1 1/2 oz/1/4 cup) **pine nuts**, toasted

1/4 teaspoon **ground allspice**

1/4 teaspoon **ground cinnamon**

1 tablespoon **lemon juice**

Sprinkle the yeast and sugar over 60 ml (2 fl oz/1/4 cup) warm water in a small bowl. Stir to dissolve the sugar, then leave in a draught-free place for 10 minutes, or until the yeast is foamy.

Put the flour and 1 teaspoon salt into the bowl of an electric mixer with a dough hook attachment and make a well in the centre. Pour the yeast mixture into the well, then, with the mixer set to the lowest speed, gradually add 250 ml (9 fl oz/ 1 cup) water and the oil, mixing for 3 minutes, or until a dough forms. Increase the speed to medium and knead for another 10 minutes, or until the dough is smooth and elastic. Alternatively, mix the dough by hand using a wooden spoon, then turn out onto a floured work surface and knead for 10 minutes, or until the dough is smooth and elastic.

Grease a large bowl with oil, then transfer the dough to the bowl, turning the dough to coat in the oil. Cover with plastic wrap and leave to rise in a draught-free place for 11/2–2 hours, or until the dough has doubled in size.

Meanwhile, prepare the topping. Heat the oil in a frying pan over medium heat. Add the onion and cook for 5 minutes, or until softened, then add the garlic and lamb and cook for 5 minutes, stirring, until browned. Add the tomatoes, pine nuts, spices and lemon juice and season to taste. Remove from the heat and cool.

Preheat oven to 220°C (425°F/Gas 7) and grease three baking trays. Knock back the dough by punching it gently, then turn out onto a floured work surface and divide into six equal portions. Shape each portion into a ball and then roll each ball out until 5 mm (1/4 inch) thick. Transfer the pizzas bases to the baking trays. Divide the topping between the pizzas, leaving a 1 cm (1/2 inch) border around the edges.

Bake the pizzas, one tray at a time, for 10–12 minutes, or until the edges are golden and the base is crisp. Serve immediately with lemon wedges and yoghurt.

Cook the **garlic and lamb** until browned, then add the **tomatoes**.

Spread the **topping** over the top of the **pizza bases**, leaving a border around the edge.

dried tomato and rosemary fougasse

makes 8

1 1/2 teaspoons (4 1/2 g) **instant dried yeast**

a pinch of **caster (superfine) sugar**

1 1/2 teaspoons **sea salt flakes**

2 1/2 tablespoons **oil** from the sun-dried tomatoes, or **extra virgin olive oil**, plus extra for brushing

2 teaspoons finely chopped **rosemary**

150 g (5 1/2 oz) **sun-dried tomatoes,** drained well (oil reserved) and patted dry

450 g (1 lb/3 2/3 cups) **plain (all-purpose) flour**

Sprinkle the yeast and sugar over 125 ml (4 fl oz/1/2 cup) warm water in a small bowl. Stir to dissolve the sugar, then leave in a draught-free place for 10 minutes, or until the yeast is foamy.

Transfer the mixture to the bowl of an electric mixer. Add another 185 ml (6 fl oz/3/4 cup) warm water, sea salt and remaining ingredients, then, using a low speed, mix for 7 minutes, or until the dough is smooth and elastic (the dough will be quite soft). Cover the bowl with a damp cloth and leave to rise in a draught-free place for 1 1/2–2 hours, or until the dough has doubled in size.

Knock back the dough by punching it gently, then turn out onto a floured work surface and cut into eight even-sized pieces. Using a floured rolling pin, roll out each piece to form an 18 x 9 cm (7 x 3 1/2 inch) oval shape. Place the fougasse on a board and, using a sharp knife, cut angled slits down each half of the oval, cutting through to the board (do not cut through the edges of the dough). Gently pull the cuts apart to form long gaps. Transfer to two greased baking trays, brush with olive oil, then cover loosely with a damp cloth. Leave for 20–25 minutes, or until slightly risen and puffy. Meanwhile, preheat the oven to 200°C (400°F/Gas 6).

Bake for 20 minutes, or until golden and crisp. Transfer to a wire rack to cool.

chocolate bread

makes two 20 cm (8 inch) loaves

2¹/2 teaspoons (7 g) **instant dried yeast**

55 g (2 oz/¹/4 cup) **caster (superfine) sugar**

90 g (3¹/4 oz) **dark chocolate**, roughly chopped

50 g (1³/4 oz) **unsalted butter**

375 g (13 oz/3 cups) **white bread (strong) flour**

30 g (1 oz/¹/4 cup) **unsweetened cocoa powder**

1 **egg**, lightly beaten

¹/2 teaspoon **natural vanilla extract**

90 g (3¹/4 oz/¹/2 cup) **dark chocolate chips**

Melt the **chocolate** and butter over a saucepan of **simmering** water.

Scatter the chocolate chips over **the dough**, then **roll it up** to form a log.

Sprinkle the yeast and a pinch of the sugar over 185 ml (6 fl oz/3/4 cup) warm water in a small bowl. Stir to dissolve the sugar, then leave in a draught-free place for 10 minutes, or until the yeast is foamy.

Put the chocolate and butter in a heatproof bowl. Sit the bowl over a saucepan of simmering water, stirring frequently until the chocolate and butter have melted. Take care that the base of the bowl doesn't touch the water.

Combine the flour, cocoa powder, 1/4 teaspoon salt and the remaining sugar in the bowl of an electric mixer with a dough hook attachment. Combine the egg and vanilla with the chocolate and butter, then pour the chocolate and yeast mixtures into the flour mixture. With the mixer set to the lowest speed, mix for 1–2 minutes, or until a dough forms. Increase the speed to medium and knead the dough for another 10 minutes, or until the dough is smooth and elastic. Alternatively, mix the dough by hand using a wooden spoon, then turn out onto a floured work surface and knead for 10 minutes, or until the dough is smooth and elastic.

Grease a large bowl with oil, then transfer the dough to the bowl, turning the dough to coat in the oil. Cover with plastic wrap and leave to rise in a draught-free place for 1 1/2–2 hours, or until the dough has doubled in size.

Knock back the dough by punching it gently, then turn out onto a floured work surface. Divide the dough in half. Gently press out each half until 1 cm (1/2 inch) thick, then scatter the chocolate chips over each. Roll up each piece of dough to form a log. Transfer to a greased baking tray. Cover with a damp cloth and leave for 1 hour, or until doubled in size. Meanwhile, preheat the oven to 180°C (350°F/Gas 4).

Bake for 45–50 minutes, or until the bread is light brown and sounds hollow when tapped on the base. Transfer to a wire rack to cool. This chocolate bread is not overly sweet, so serve freshly sliced or toasted with sweetened mascarpone.

fruit and tea loaf

makes one 25 x 11 cm (10 x 4¼ inch) loaf

500 g (1 lb 2 oz/2¾ cups) **mixed dried fruit**

185 ml (6 fl oz/¾ cup) strong, hot **black tea**

125 g (4½ oz/⅔ cup) lightly packed **soft brown sugar**

1 **egg**, lightly beaten

125 g (4½ oz/1 cup) **plain (all-purpose) flour**

¾ teaspoon **baking powder**

1 teaspoon **ground cinnamon**

¼ teaspoon **ground nutmeg**

a large pinch of **ground cloves**

Combine the fruit and hot tea in a large bowl, cover with plastic wrap and leave for 3 hours or overnight.

Preheat the oven to 160°C (315°F/Gas 2–3). Grease a 25 x 11 cm (10 x 4¼ inch) loaf tin and line the base with baking paper. Dust the sides of the tin with a little flour, shaking off any excess.

Stir the sugar and egg into the fruit mixture to combine well. Sift the flour, baking powder and spices into a bowl, then add the fruit mixture. Using a large slotted spoon, stir to combine well.

Spoon the mixture into the tin and bake for 1 hour 35 minutes, covering the top with foil if it browns too quickly. The loaf is cooked when a skewer inserted into the centre of the loaf comes out clean. Cool the loaf in the tin, then turn out and serve, sliced and buttered, if desired.

The loaf will keep, wrapped in plastic wrap and stored in an airtight container in a cool place, for up to 1 week, or up to 8 weeks in the freezer.

greek lemon, dill and feta bread

makes two 20 x 10 cm (8 x 4 inch) loaves

375 g (13 oz/3 cups) **white bread (strong) flour**

125 g (4¹/2 oz/1 cup) **semolina**

1 tablespoon (12 g) **instant dried yeast**

1 teaspoon **caster (superfine) sugar**

2 tablespoons **olive oil**

60 g (2¹/4 oz/1 bunch) **dill**, finely chopped

grated **zest** from 1 **lemon**

200 g (7 oz/1¹/3 cups) coarsely crumbled **feta cheese**, well drained

Combine the flour, semolina, yeast, sugar and 1¹/2 teaspoons salt in the bowl of an electric mixer with a dough hook attachment and make a well in the centre. Pour 250 ml (9 fl oz/1 cup) warm water and the oil into the well. With the mixer set to the lowest speed, mix for 3 minutes, or until a dough forms. Increase the speed to medium, add the dill and lemon zest and knead for another 8 minutes, or until the dough is smooth and elastic. Add the feta and knead for 2 minutes, or until the feta is incorporated into the dough.

Alternatively, mix the dough by hand using a wooden spoon, then turn out onto a floured work surface, sprinkle over the dill and lemon zest and knead for 8 minutes or until the dill and zest are incorporated and the dough is smooth and elastic. Pat the dough into a rectangle approximately 20 x 10 cm (8 x 4 inches) and sprinkle over the feta. Fold the dough over several times, then knead for 2 minutes, or until the feta is incorporated.

Grease a large bowl with oil, then transfer the dough to the bowl, turning the dough to coat in the oil. Cover with plastic wrap and leave to rise in a draught-free place for 1¹/2–2 hours, or until the dough has doubled in size.

Knock back the dough by punching it gently, then turn out onto a floured work surface. Divide the dough in half and form each into a loaf shape and place, seam side down, into two greased 20 x 10 cm (8 x 4 inch) loaf tins. Cover with a damp cloth and leave for 30 minutes, or until doubled in size. Meanwhile, preheat the oven to 200°C (400°F/Gas 6). Bake the bread for 10 minutes, then reduce the oven to 180°C (350°F/Gas 4) and bake for a further 20 minutes, or until golden and sounds hollow when tapped on the base. Transfer to a wire rack to cool.

sardine and silverbeet wholemeal pizza

makes two 30 cm (12 inch) pizzas

2 teaspoons (6 g) **instant dried yeast**
a pinch of **caster (superfine) sugar**
300 g (10½ oz/2⅓ cups) **white bread (strong) flour**
115 g (4 oz/¾ cup) **wholemeal (whole-wheat) flour**
1½ teaspoons **sea salt flakes**
2½ tablespoons **olive oil**

topping

2½ tablespoons **extra virgin olive oil**
1 large **onion**, peeled and finely chopped
5 **garlic cloves**, peeled and thinly sliced
1 bunch **silverbeet (Swiss chard)**, stems removed and discarded, leaves washed, dried and chopped
85 g (3 oz/⅔ cup) **raisins**, roughly chopped
150 g (5½ oz/1½ cups) grated **parmesan cheese**
a large pinch of **chilli flakes**, or to taste
2 x 100 g (3½ oz) tins **sardines in oil**, drained

Add the **silverbeet** and raisins to the saucepan, then **cover** and cook until the silverbeet has wilted.

Divide **the topping** between the two pizzas **and arrange** the sardines over the top.

Sprinkle the yeast and sugar over 60 ml (2 fl oz/1/4 cup) warm water in a small bowl. Stir to dissolve the sugar, then leave in a draught-free place for 10 minutes, or until the yeast is foamy.

Put the white bread and wholemeal flours and sea salt into the bowl of an electric mixer with a dough hook attachment and make a well in the centre. Pour the yeast mixture into the well, then, with the mixer set to the lowest speed, gradually add 250 ml (9 fl oz/1 cup) warm water and the olive oil, mixing for 3 minutes, or until a soft dough forms. Increase the speed to medium and knead for 7 minutes, or until the dough is smooth and elastic (the dough will be very soft). Alternatively, mix the dough by hand using a wooden spoon, then turn out onto a floured work surface and knead for 7 minutes, or until the dough is smooth and elastic.

Grease a large bowl with oil, then transfer the dough to the bowl, turning the dough to coat in the oil. Cover with plastic wrap and leave to rise in a draught-free place for 11/2 hours, or until the dough has doubled in size.

Meanwhile, to make the topping, heat the oil in a large saucepan. Add the onion and garlic and stir over medium–high heat for 3 minutes, or until soft and light golden. Add the silverbeet and raisins, cover, then cook for 3 minutes, stirring often, or until the silverbeet has wilted. Remove from the heat and cool slightly, then stir in the parmesan and chilli flakes and season with salt and pepper.

Preheat the oven to 220°C (425°F/Gas 7). Lightly grease two 30 cm (12 inch) pizza trays. Alternatively, the pizzas can be baked directly on a pizza stone.

Knock back the dough by punching it gently, then turn out onto a floured work surface. Cut the dough in half and roll out each half to form a circle, approximately 30 cm (12 inches) in diameter. Transfer to the trays. Divide the silverbeet mixture between the pizza bases, scattering to cover, then top with sardines. Bake for 15–20 minutes, or until the bases are crisp and golden. Serve hot.

tahini spirals

makes 10

1 teaspoon (3 g) **instant dried yeast**

1 teaspoon **caster (superfine) sugar**

1 tablespoon **olive oil**

335 g (11¾ oz/2⅔ cups) **white bread (strong) flour**

90 g (3¼ oz/⅓ cup) **tahini**

60 g (2¼ oz/⅓ cup) **soft brown sugar**

2 teaspoons **vegetable oil**

Sprinkle the yeast and sugar over 250 ml (9 fl oz/1 cup) warm water in a large bowl. Stir to dissolve the sugar, then leave in a draught-free place for 10 minutes, or until the yeast is foamy, then stir in the olive oil.

Combine the yeast mixture and a third of the flour in the bowl of an electric mixer with a dough hook attachment. With the mixer set to the lowest speed, gradually add the remaining flour, 60 g (2¼ oz/½ cup) at a time, mixing until a dough forms. Increase the speed to medium and knead for 7 minutes, or until the dough is smooth and elastic. Alternatively, mix the dough by hand using a wooden spoon, then turn out onto a floured work surface and knead the dough for 7 minutes, or until smooth and elastic.

Grease a large bowl with oil, then transfer the dough to the bowl, turning the dough to coat in the oil. Cover with plastic wrap and leave to rise in a draught-free place for 2 hours, or until the dough has doubled in size.

Preheat the oven to 190°C (375°F/Gas 5). Lightly grease two baking trays. Put the tahini, brown sugar and vegetable oil in a small bowl, stirring to mix well.

Knock back the dough by punching it gently, then turn out onto a floured work surface and divide into 10 equal portions. Working with one portion at a time, roll each to form a 20 x 10 cm (8 x 4 inch) rectangle. Spread about 1 tablespoon of tahini mixture over the dough, spreading it to the edges. Starting at the long edge of the rectangle, roll it up to form a long cylinder. Tightly coil the cylinder to form a round, then tuck the end underneath. Transfer the spirals to the prepared baking trays and, using the palm of your hand, flatten slightly. Bake for 12–15 minutes, or until golden. Serve warm or at room temperature.

walnut and cheddar soda bread

makes one 20 cm (8 inch) round loaf

250 g (9 oz/2 cups) **plain (all-purpose) flour**

225 g (8 oz/1 1/2 cups) **wholemeal (whole-wheat) flour**

1 tablespoon **baking powder**

1 teaspoon **bicarbonate of soda (baking soda)**

1 tablespoon **soft brown sugar**

60 g (2 1/4 oz/1/2 cup) **walnut pieces,** chopped

175 g (6 oz/1 1/2 cups) grated **mature cheddar cheese**

40 g (1 1/2 oz) **butter**, melted and cooled

2 **eggs**, lightly beaten

250 ml (9 fl oz/1 cup) **buttermilk**

Preheat the oven to 180°C (350°F/Gas 4). Line a baking tray with baking paper.

Sift the flours, baking powder and bicarbonate of soda into a large bowl (tip any husks from the wholemeal flour left in the sieve back into the mixture). Stir in the sugar, walnuts and cheese. Make a well in the centre. Combine the butter, eggs and buttermilk in a bowl and pour into the well. Stir with a wooden spoon until a soft dough forms, then turn out onto a lightly floured work surface. Using lightly floured hands, knead briefly just until smooth, then shape the dough into a 20 cm (8 inch) round. Transfer to the baking tray.

Using a sharp, lightly floured knife, cut a 1 cm (1/2 inch) deep cross into the top of the loaf. Bake for 30–40 minutes, or until golden.

tip For a variation, replace the cheddar cheese with 100 g (3 1/2 oz/1/2 cup) chopped dried pear and 1 teaspoon aniseed. Bake as above and serve warm, with cheese.

hot cross buns

makes 16

1 tablespoon (12 g) **instant dried yeast**

80 g (2³/4 oz/1/3 cup) **caster (superfine) sugar**

625 g (1 lb 6 oz/5 cups) **white bread (strong) flour**

1¹/2 teaspoons **mixed (pumpkin pie) spice**

1 teaspoon **ground cinnamon**

1 teaspoon **ground nutmeg**

250 ml (9 fl oz/1 cup) **warm milk**

100 g (3¹/2 oz) **unsalted butter**, melted

2 **eggs**, lightly beaten

200 g (7 oz/1¹/3 cups) **currants**

70 g (2¹/2 oz/1/3 cup) **mixed peel**

glaze

2 tablespoons **caster (superfine) sugar**

cross dough

60 g (2¹/4 oz/1/2 cup) **plain (all-purpose) flour**

If making the dough by hand, **turn out** onto a floured surface and **knead** until the dough is smooth.

Brush the **dough** strips with water. Place two strips **on each bun** to form a cross.

Sprinkle the yeast and a pinch of the sugar over 125 ml (4 fl oz/1/2 cup) warm water in a small bowl. Stir to dissolve the sugar, then leave in a draught-free place for 10 minutes, or until the yeast is foamy.

Combine the flour, spices and 1/2 teaspoon salt in a bowl and set aside.

Combine the milk, butter, remaining sugar, eggs and 125 g (41/2 oz/1 cup) of the flour mixture in the bowl of an electric mixer with a dough hook attachment. Mix for 1 minute, or until smooth. Add the yeast mixture, currants and mixed peel and stir to combine. Add the flour, 125 g (41/2 oz/1 cup) at a time, stirring to mix well after each addition. As the dough becomes sticky and more difficult to mix, use the lowest speed and knead for 5 minutes. Alternatively, mix the dough by hand using a wooden spoon, then turn out onto a lightly floured work surface and knead for 5 minutes, or until the dough is smooth and elastic.

Grease a large bowl with oil, then transfer the dough to the bowl, turning the dough to coat in the oil. Cover with plastic wrap and leave to rise in a draught-free place for 11/2–2 hours, or until the dough has doubled in size.

Knock back the dough by punching it gently, then turn out onto a floured work surface. Divide the dough into 16 equal portions. Roll each portion into a ball, then place on greased baking trays, spacing the rolls about 4 cm (11/2 inches) apart. Cover with a damp cloth and leave for 30 minutes, or until doubled in size.

Preheat the oven to 180°C (350°F/Gas 4). To make the glaze, combine the sugar with 2 tablespoons water in a small saucepan. Bring slowly to the boil over high heat, then remove from the heat and set aside.

To prepare the cross dough, put the flour in a small bowl and gradually add 60 ml (2 fl oz/1/4 cup) water, stirring to form a dough. Roll out the dough on a floured work surface to a 2 mm (1/16 inch) thickness. Cut into 5 mm (1/4 inch) wide strips, about 12 cm (41/2 inches) long. Brush the strips with water and place two strips over each bun to form a cross. Bake the buns for 15–20 minutes, or until golden brown. Brush the hot buns with the glaze and transfer to a wire rack to cool.

oatmeal and raspberry muffins

makes 12 muffins

125 g (4¹/2 oz/1 cup) **medium oatmeal**

375 ml (13 fl oz/1¹/2 cups) **milk**

250 g (9 oz/2 cups) **plain (all-purpose) flour**

1 tablespoon **baking powder**

115 g (4 oz/¹/2 cup) **soft brown sugar**

1 **egg**, lightly beaten

90 g (3¹/4 oz/¹/4 cup) **honey**

60 g (2¹/4 oz) **unsalted butter**, melted

150 g (5¹/2 oz/1¹/4 cups) **raspberries**

Preheat the oven to 190°C (375°F/Gas 5). Grease a 12-hole standard muffin tin, or line the holes with paper cases.

Put the oatmeal in a bowl, stir in the milk and set aside for 5 minutes. Sift the flour and baking powder into a large bowl, then stir in the sugar. Make a well in the centre.

Combine the egg, honey and butter in a bowl and stir to mix well. Pour the egg mixture and oatmeal mixture into the well, then stir quickly until just combined. Do not overmix — the batter will still be slightly lumpy. Gently fold in the raspberries.

Divide the mixture evenly between the muffin holes. Bake for 20–25 minutes, or until the muffins are golden and a skewer inserted into the centre of a muffin comes out clean. Cool for 5 minutes before transferring to a wire rack. Serve warm.

tip Softer batter mixes, such as muffin batter, should not be overworked or the muffins will be tough and rubbery. Stir the mixture gently with a metal spoon until just combined.

low-fat apricot and orange muffins

makes 12 muffins

140 g (5 oz/3/4 cup) **dried apricots,** roughly chopped

grated **zest** from 1 **orange**

125 ml (4 fl oz/1/2 cup) freshly squeezed **orange juice**

250 g (9 oz/2 cups) **self-raising flour**

175 g (6 oz/1/2 cup) **honey**

30 g (1 oz) **unsalted butter**, melted

185 ml (6 fl oz/3/4 cup) **skim milk**

1 **egg**, lightly beaten

Preheat the oven to 180°C (350°F/Gas 4). Grease a 12-hole standard muffin tin, or line the holes with paper cases.

Combine the apricots, orange zest and juice in a small saucepan and cook over medium heat until just warmed through. Remove from the heat and cool.

Sift the flour into a large bowl and make a well in the centre. Combine the honey, butter, milk and egg in a bowl, stirring to mix well. Pour into the well, then add the apricot mixture and stir quickly until just combined. Do not overmix — the batter will still be slightly lumpy.

Divide the mixture evenly between the muffin holes. Bake for 20–25 minutes, or until golden and a skewer inserted into the centre of a muffin comes out clean. Cool in the tin for 2 minutes before transferring to a wire rack.

tip When making muffins, always sift the flour. This will aerate the flour and ensure a light muffin.

apple, buttermilk, maple syrup and bran muffins

makes 12 muffins

70 g (2¹/2 oz/1 cup) **unprocessed bran**

375 ml (13 fl oz/1¹/2 cups) **buttermilk**

185 ml (6 fl oz/³/4 cup) **maple syrup**

1 **egg**, lightly beaten

60 ml (2 fl oz/¹/4 cup) **vegetable oil**

1 **cooking apple** (such as granny smith), peeled, cored and chopped

70 g (2¹/2 oz/¹/2 cup) **hazelnuts**, toasted, peeled (see tip, below) and chopped

250 g (9 oz/2 cups) **self-raising flour**

1 teaspoon **ground cinnamon**

Preheat the oven to 180°C (350°F/Gas 4). Grease a 12-hole standard muffin tin, or line the holes with paper cases.

Combine the bran and buttermilk in a bowl, stirring to mix well, then set aside for 5 minutes. Add the maple syrup, egg, oil, apple and hazelnuts and stir to combine well. Sift the flour and cinnamon over the mixture, then gently fold in until just combined. Do not overmix — the batter will still be slightly lumpy.

Divide the mixture evenly between the muffin holes. Bake for 20–25 minutes, or until golden and a skewer inserted into the centre of a muffin comes out clean. Cool in the tin for 2 minutes before transferring to a wire rack.

tip To toast the hazelnuts, put them in a single layer on a large baking tray. Toast either in the oven at 180°C (350°F/Gas 4) or under a preheated grill (broiler) for about 2 minutes (turn them after 1 minute and watch carefully, as nuts burn quickly). Tip into a tea towel (dish towel) and rub the skins off. Not all the skins will come off entirely; don't worry about those that don't.

polenta, semi-dried tomato, pecorino and basil muffins

makes 12 muffins or 48 mini muffins

155 g (5½ oz/1¼ cups) **self-raising flour**

110 g (3¾ oz/¾ cup) **polenta (cornmeal)**

60 g (2¼ oz/¾ cup) grated **pecorino cheese**

1 **egg**, lightly beaten

250 ml (9 fl oz/1 cup) **milk**

80 ml (2½ fl oz/⅓ cup) **olive oil**

40 g (1½ oz/¼ cup) chopped **semi-dried (sun-blushed) tomatoes**

15 g (½ oz/¼ cup) chopped **basil**

Preheat the oven to 180°C (350°F/Gas 4). Grease a 12-hole standard muffin tin or two 24-hole mini muffin tins, or line the holes with paper cases.

Sift the flour into a large bowl, then stir in the polenta and pecorino and season with freshly ground black pepper. Make a well in the centre. Combine the egg, milk and oil in a bowl, then pour into the well. Add the tomatoes and basil and stir quickly until just combined. Do not overmix — the batter will still be slightly lumpy.

Divide the mixture evenly between the muffin holes. Bake for 20–25 minutes (or 10–12 minutes for mini muffins), or until the muffins are golden and come away from the sides of the tin. Cool in the tin for 2 minutes before transferring to a wire rack. Serve warm.

tip Most muffins should be left to cool for a few minutes in the tins once out of the oven. Don't leave them for too long or trapped steam will make the bases soggy.

sweet yoghurt plait

makes 2 loaves

650 g (1 lb 7 oz/5¼ cups) **white bread (strong) flour**
1 tablespoon **ground cinnamon**
3 teaspoons (9 g) **instant dried yeast**
2 **eggs**, lightly beaten
250 g (9 oz/1 cup) **Greek-style yoghurt**
125 ml (4 fl oz/½ cup) **lukewarm milk**
90 g (3¼ oz/¼ cup) **honey**
60 g (2¼ oz) **butter**, chopped
100 g (3½ oz/½ cup) chopped **dried figs**

glaze
1 **egg**
2 tablespoons **milk**

icing
375 g (13 oz/3 cups) **icing (confectioners') sugar**, sifted
80 ml (2½ fl oz/⅓ cup) **lemon juice**

Add the **butter and figs** and mix for another 10 minutes.

For each loaf, plait together **three lengths** of dough. Tuck the ends underneath **to neaten**.

Combine 600 g (1 lb 5 oz/4³/4 cups) of the flour, cinnamon, yeast and 1 teaspoon salt in the bowl of an electric mixer with a dough hook attachment and make a well in the centre. Combine the eggs, yoghurt, milk and honey in a bowl, then pour into the well. With the mixer set to the lowest speed, mix for 3 minutes to combine well. Increase the speed to medium and add the butter and figs and knead for 10 minutes, or until the dough is smooth and elastic; add the remaining flour if the mixture is still sticky. Alternatively, mix the dough by hand, using a wooden spoon, then turn out onto a lightly floured work surface and knead for 10 minutes, or until smooth and elastic.

Grease a large bowl with oil, then transfer the dough to the bowl, turning the dough to coat in the oil. Cover with plastic wrap and leave to rise in a draught-free place for 1 1/2 hours, or until the dough has doubled in size.

Knock back the dough by punching it gently, then turn out onto a floured work surface. Cut the dough into six equal portions, then roll each into 30 cm (12 inch) lengths. Plait three lengths of dough together, tucking the ends underneath for a neat finish. Repeat with the remaining dough lengths to make a second loaf.

Transfer to a large, lightly greased baking tray. Cover the tray with a damp cloth and leave for 30 minutes, or until the dough has doubled in size. Meanwhile, preheat the oven to 220°C (425°F/Gas 7).

To make the glaze, mix together the egg and milk and brush over the tops of the loaves. Bake for 10 minutes, then reduce the oven to 180°C (350°F/Gas 4) and bake for a further 20 minutes, or until the bread is golden and sounds hollow when tapped on the base. If the loaves start to brown too quickly, cover them with foil. Transfer to a wire rack to cool.

To make the icing, combine the icing sugar, lemon juice and 2 tablespoons boiling water in a bowl and, using a fork, stir until smooth. Drizzle over the cooled loaves. Set aside until the icing has set.

yorkshire puddings

makes 6

170 ml (5¹/2 fl oz/²/3 cup) **milk**

2 **eggs**

85 g (3 oz/²/3 cup) **plain (all-purpose) flour**

125 ml (4 fl oz/¹/2 cup) **vegetable oil**

Preheat the oven to 220°C (425°F/Gas 7). Whisk the milk and eggs together in a bowl. Sift the flour over the milk mixture, then whisk to form a smooth batter.

Divide the oil between six holes of a 12-hole standard muffin tin. Place the tin in the oven for 3 minutes, or until the oil is very hot. Spoon the batter into the prepared muffin holes until three-quarters full, then bake for 15 minutes, or until the puddings are puffed and golden. Remove from the tin and serve immediately. Traditionally Yorkshire puddings are served with roast beef and gravy.

tip For well-risen, light Yorkshire puddings, the oil in the tin should be heated until very hot — almost smoking — otherwise, the puddings will not rise.

plum and rosemary flat bread

makes one 25 cm (10 inch) round bread

60 ml (2 fl oz/1/4 cup) **warm milk**

2 teaspoons (6 g) **instant dried yeast**

115 g (4 oz/1/2 cup) **caster (superfine) sugar**

2 **eggs**, lightly beaten

grated **zest** from 1 **lemon**

2 teaspoons finely chopped **rosemary**

185 g (61/2 oz/11/2 cups) **white bread (strong) flour**

150 g (51/2 oz) **unsalted butter**, softened, cut into pieces

10 **plums**, halved and stoned, or 800 g (1 lb 12 oz) **tinned plums**, drained

whipped cream or **mascarpone**, to serve

Grease a 25 cm (10 inch) spring-form cake tin or a loose-based flan tin with butter.

Combine the milk and yeast in the bowl of an electric mixer. Stir in 55 g (2 oz/1/4 cup) of the sugar, eggs, lemon zest and 1 teaspoon of the rosemary, then add the flour. Using the beater attachment, mix for 1 minute, or until a soft dough forms. Add the butter, then continue mixing for a further minute, or until the dough is smooth, shiny and thick. Alternatively, mix the dough by hand using a wooden spoon.

Spoon into the prepared tin and cover with plastic wrap. Leave in a draught-free place for 11/2–2 hours, or until doubled in size.

Knock back the dough by punching it gently. Dampen the palms of your hands with water and press the dough into the edges of the tin. Arrange the plums, cut side up, over the top, pressing them gently into the dough. Leave for 30 minutes. Meanwhile, preheat the oven to 200°C (400°F/Gas 6).

Sprinkle the plums with the remaining sugar and scatter over the remaining rosemary. Bake for 10 minutes, then reduce the oven to 180°C (350°F/Gas 4) and bake for a further 20 minutes, or until light golden and slightly spongy when pressed in the centre. Serve warm, cut into wedges, with cream or mascarpone.

parmesan grissini

makes 32

1 teaspoon (3 g) **instant dried yeast**

a pinch of **caster (superfine) sugar**

1 tablespoon **extra virgin olive oil**

250 g (9 oz/2 cups) **white bread (strong) flour**

60 g (2¼ oz/⅔ cup) grated **parmesan cheese**

Sprinkle the yeast and sugar over 170 ml (5½ fl oz/⅔ cup) warm water in a small bowl. Stir to dissolve the sugar, then leave in a draught-free place for 10 minutes, or until the yeast is foamy. Stir in the olive oil.

Put the flour in a large bowl, add the parmesan and 1 teaspoon salt and stir to combine well. Pour in the yeast mixture and stir until a dough forms. Turn the dough out onto a lightly floured work surface and knead for 5 minutes, or until the dough is smooth and elastic.

Grease a large bowl with oil, then transfer the dough to the bowl, turning the dough to coat in the oil. Cover with plastic wrap and leave to rise in a draught-free place for 1 hour, or until the dough has doubled in size.

Preheat the oven to 200°C (400°F/Gas 6). Lightly grease two baking trays. Knock back the dough by punching it gently, then turn out onto a floured work surface and cut in half. Roll out one piece of dough to form a 20 x 16 cm (8 x 6¼ inch) rectangle, then cut into sixteen 1 cm (½ inch) wide strips. Using your hands, gently roll each strip to form a 22–24 cm (8½–9½ inch) long stick, then place on the baking tray. Repeat for the second piece of dough. Bake for 17–20 minutes, or until golden and crisp, swapping the trays halfway through to ensure even cooking. Transfer to a wire rack to cool.

Grissini will keep, stored in an airtight container, for up to 7 days. Re-crisp in a 180°C (350°F/Gas 4) oven for 5 minutes if they become soft.

orange and blueberry rolls

makes 20 rolls

1 tablespoon (12 g) **instant dried yeast**

75 g (2¹/2 oz/¹/3 cup) **caster (superfine) sugar**

250 ml (9 fl oz/1 cup) warm **milk**

125 g (4¹/2 oz) **unsalted butter**, softened

80 ml (2¹/2 fl oz/¹/3 cup) freshly squeezed **orange juice**

2 **eggs**, lightly beaten

375 g (13 oz/3 cups) **white bread (strong) flour**

icing (confectioners') sugar, for dusting

filling

100 g (3¹/2 oz) **unsalted butter**, softened

115 g (4 oz/¹/2 cup) **caster (superfine) sugar**

grated **zest** from 2 **oranges**

270 g (9¹/2 oz/1³/4 cups) **blueberries**

Sprinkle the yeast and a pinch of the sugar over 100 ml (3½ fl oz) warm milk in a small bowl. Stir to dissolve the sugar, then leave in a draught-free place for 10 minutes, or until the yeast is foamy.

Put the remaining milk and sugar, the butter and 1 teaspoon salt in the bowl of an electric mixer. Using the beater attachment, mix until the butter has just melted. Add the orange juice, eggs and yeast mixture and mix to combine. Using the lowest speed, gradually add the flour, 60 g (2¼ oz/½ cup) at a time, mixing until the dough is soft and smooth.

Grease a large bowl with oil, then transfer the dough to the bowl, turning the dough to coat in the oil. Cover with plastic wrap and leave to rise in a draught-free place for 1 hour, or until the dough has doubled in size.

To make the filling, cream the butter, sugar and orange zest in a small bowl using electric beaters until pale and fluffy. Grease two 20 cm (8 inch) round spring-form cake tins.

Turn the dough out onto a lightly floured work surface and divide in half. Roll each piece into a 25 x 15 cm (10 x 6 inch) rectangle. Spread half the filling mixture over one rectangle, then arrange half the blueberries over the top. Repeat with the remaining rectangle of dough, filling and blueberries. Starting from the long side, roll up each rectangle to form a cylinder. Then, using a lightly floured, serrated knife, cut each cylinder into 10 equal rolls. Arrange 10 rolls, cut side up, over the base of each tin. Cover with a damp cloth and leave for 45 minutes, or until the rolls have doubled in size. Meanwhile, preheat the oven to 180°C (350°F/Gas 4).

Bake the rolls for 25–30 minutes, or until the rolls are golden and come away from the sides of the tins. Cool in the tins for 5 minutes, then transfer to a wire rack to cool. Dust with icing sugar to serve.

Scatter the blueberries **over the** filling and roll up to form a **cylinder**.

Arrange the rolls, **cut side up**, over the base of each tin.

cheese pinwheel scones

makes 10

250 g (9 oz/2 cups) **plain (all-purpose) flour**

1 tablespoon **baking powder**

1/8 teaspoon **cayenne pepper**

30 g (1 oz) **unsalted butter**, chilled and diced

185 ml (6 fl oz/3/4 cup) **milk**

filling

40 g (11/2 oz/1/4 cup) **goat's cheese**, crumbled

40 g (11/2 oz/1/2 cup) grated **parmesan cheese**

40 g (11/2 oz/1/3 cup) grated **mature cheddar cheese**

2 tablespoons chopped **flat-leaf (Italian) parsley**

Preheat the oven to 220°C (425°F/Gas 7). Grease or line a baking tray.

Sift the flour, baking powder, a pinch of salt and cayenne into a large mixing bowl. Using your fingertips, rub in the butter until the mixture resembles breadcrumbs. Add the milk and, using a flat-bladed knife, mix to form a soft dough. Add a little extra flour if the dough is too sticky.

Turn the dough out onto a floured work surface and roll out to form a 20 x 25 cm (8 x 10 inch) rectangle. Sprinkle the goat's cheese over the surface, then sprinkle over the parmesan, cheddar and parsley. Starting from the long side, roll the dough into a cylinder. Cut the cylinder into 10 equal 2 cm (3/4 inch) thick slices. Transfer the slices to a baking tray, spacing them 2 cm (3/4 inch) apart.

Bake for 10–12 minutes, or until golden and cooked through. Cool on a wire rack. Serve warm.

cakes

about cakes

Although the word 'cake' derives from a Viking word *kaka*, the art of cake-making can be traced back to ancient Egypt, where royal bakers were depicted in carvings on the tombs of pharaohs. Their cakes were, in fact, leavened breads enriched with honey, nuts and spices. It was the addition of eggs and butter to bread dough by the Romans that produced a more open, porous texture, giving a clearer distinction between the two.

Trade played a huge part in the development of cakes. Sugar was brought from northern India, nuts and spices from the Middle East and, in the 16th century, the Spanish returned from Mexico with chocolate. These developments weren't restricted to ingredients: cake hoops were invented, and moulded cakes began to replace freeform types. But it was the technology of the 19th century that saw the greatest breakthrough — the invention of bicarbonate of soda (baking soda) and baking powder — which dramatically changed the way cakes were baked.

cakes today

Today, home baking is part of almost every culture. Home-baked cakes come in a myriad of shapes, sizes, textures and flavours and we love them all for their sweet indulgence.

There are three major methods for mixing a cake and each one produces a cake with a slightly different texture. Creamed cakes, with their high percentage of fat, have a short, soft crumb. Whisked cakes are made with lots of eggs, which aerate the batter. They tend to rise dramatically in the oven and although they fall back a little once cooked their texture remains light and fluffy. Cakes made using the melt-and-mix method, where the butter and sugar are melted together, produces a particularly moist, dense crumb. Often highly spiced, these wonderfully moist cakes keep well and the flavour improves with time.

To bake a great cake, you need good quality ingredients. Beyond the basics there is an almost endless list of flavourings that can be added to give a cake its character. Cakes can be small, grand, delicate, moist or dense. They can be enriched with dried fruits and nuts, sliced and filled with flavoured creams and fresh fruit, and they can even be healthy. We bake cakes in tins of varying shapes and sizes. A sponge cake is usually made in two shallow tins, the resulting cake layered with cream, jam and soft fruits. Rich fruit cakes are baked in deep cake tins, double-lined with baking paper to protect the cake from scorching during the longer baking times. There are tins, some quite decorative, with wonderful names like kugelhopf and bundt, originating in Central Europe but now popular all over. Small cakes are cooked in individual cake tins, such as friand tins or timbale moulds.

Cake-making is a symbol of celebration: we bake them for parties, weddings, birthdays, christenings and religious festivals, and yet cakes are also a symbol of an everyday celebration, as we take time out to enjoy them with a morning coffee or when friends drop by.

essential ingredients

flour

plain (all-purpose) flour: Virtually all cakes are made using wheat flour. Plain flour is made from a mixture of hard and soft wheat varieties and has a low gluten content. A high-gluten flour, such as white bread (strong) flour, would produce a tough, chewy cake.

self-raising flour: This has baking powder already added.

rice flour: Contains no gluten and is often used to soften a cake batter. It can be used exclusively or in combination with plain (all-purpose) flour.

eggs

Use 60 g (2¼ oz), or grade 3, eggs in all recipes, unless stated otherwise. Always store eggs in the refrigerator and allow them to return to room temperature before use. Discard any that appear cracked.

leaveners

bicarbonate of soda (baking soda): A chemical raising agent. This is an alkaline substance that requires an acid to kick-start it into producing enough carbon dioxide to aerate the batter. These acids are either lactic (yoghurt, sour cream or buttermilk) or acetic (lemon juice or vinegar), and as soon as they are introduced to the bicarbonate of soda and a liquid, the gases begin to work.

baking powder: Made from bicarbonate of soda and ground starch (to help absorb moisture). Baking powder works in two stages. Firstly, when it comes into contact with the batter it gives off an initial burst of gas that produces small bubbles. Secondly, when it comes into contact with the heat in the oven it produces a larger amount of carbon dioxide, which enables the cake batter to rise.

fat

Butter is the preferred fat in most forms of baking, but olive oil, vegetable oil and margarines are also used. Fat tenderizes and 'shortens' the dough and is responsible for giving cakes that melt-in-the-mouth texture we desire. Olive oil and vegetable oil add a distinctive flavour to cakes as well as producing a looser, more crumbly texture.

sweeteners

sugar: This affects the flavour, colour and texture of cakes. It sweetens a cake, tenderizes and helps draw out the moisture in a batter. All types of sugar can be used in cake-making. Soft brown sugar adds a deeper colour and slight caramel flavour to a cake.

honey, golden (or dark corn) syrup and treacle: These are all fructose sugars and give flavour and moisture to cakes.

molasses: Adds a malty flavour and deep golden colour to cakes.

additional flavourings

chocolate: Dark chocolate usually needs to be melted before it can be incorporated into a cake batter. Sometimes it may be directly grated into the batter. Always use a good-quality dark chocolate.

unsweetened cocoa powder: Needs to be sifted in with the flour and other dry ingredients.

nuts: These add flavour and texture to a cake and may also be used as an alternative to flour in some flourless cake recipes.

fruit: Dried fruits of all varieties can be used in cake-making and are sometimes soaked in alcohol before being stirred into the cake batter. Fresh fruit can be folded into or scattered over the surface of the batter prior to baking, or layered in the centre of the batter for a surprise filling. Citrus flavour is added to cakes either as finely grated zest or as juice.

before and after

preparing the tins

For some cakes, greasing and flouring the tin is sufficient to prevent the batter sticking to the tin, and for the cake to easily turn out of the tin once cooked. Use melted, unsalted butter to grease tins, unless the recipe suggests otherwise. Some cakes benefit from having a baking paper lining on the base (and, sometimes, the sides) of the tin.

lining a round cake tin: Put the tin on a sheet of baking paper and trace around the base with a pencil. Cut out the marked shape. Grease the inside of the tin and position the piece of baking paper in the base (greasing the tin first helps the baking paper to stick to the tin).

lining a loaf or rectangular cake tin: Grease the inside of the tin. Put the tin in the centre of a piece of baking paper. Make a diagonal cut from each corner of the paper to the corners of the tin. Fold the paper between the cut edges to make it easier to put into the tin. Insert the paper into the greased tin, overlapping the corners of the paper, and press to secure.

making the batter

creaming method: Using an electric mixer, cream the butter and sugar together in a bowl until pale and fluffy. Gradually beat in the eggs a little at a time until incorporated. The butter and sugar are creamed sufficiently when a spoonful of the mixture drops easily from the spoon when tapped gently. The flour and liquid are then added, sometimes in alternate batches. Transfer the batter to the prepared tin and smooth the top. Bake as directed.

whisking method: Put the whole eggs, or yolks, and the sugar into a bowl and using a balloon whisk or electric hand mixer, whisk for 5–8 minutes, or until the mixture is pale, has trebled in volume and reaches the ribbon stage (the batter will leave a thick trail when the beaters are lifted). Sift over the flour and carefully fold into the batter using a large metal spoon. Stir in melted butter, if using, and transfer to the prepared tin. Bake as directed.

melt-and-mix method: Put the butter, sugar and any liquid into a saucepan and heat gently until the butter has melted and the ingredients are combined. Allow to cool slightly. Fold the dry ingredients together and then stir in the melted mixture, along with any eggs, until evenly combined. Pour the batter into the prepared tin. Bake as directed.

baking the cake

Bake the cake on the centre shelf of the oven (unless otherwise directed) and cook for the amount of time specified. If two times are given, for example between 30 and 35 minutes, always check after 30 minutes.

testing for doneness: A cake is cooked when it starts to shrink back slightly from the edge of the tin; when pressed lightly in the centre the cake should spring back; or it can be tested with a cake tester or a metal skewer. Insert the skewer into the centre of the cake and remove it — it should be totally clean. If there is any sticky cake mixture left on the skewer, return the cake to the oven and bake for a further 5 minutes before retesting. This process can be repeated until the skewer comes out clean. This method is not suitable for cakes that contain lots of fruit or those that are meant to have a sticky texture, so follow the instructions in the recipe.

turning out: After cooking, most cakes need to be turned out of their tins. Most recipes suggest that the cake is left to cool slightly in the tin, usually for about 5 minutes. After this time the cake will have firmed up sufficiently and there won't be the risk of it cracking when turned out. Run a flat-bladed knife or palette knife gently around the edge of the cake, invert it onto a wire rack, remove the tin and carefully peel away the baking paper (if using). Leave to cool completely.

hints and tips

- Before you start baking, read the recipe thoroughly and check you have the correct quantity of ingredients and the necessary equipment.

- Bring chilled ingredients, such as butter and eggs, to room temperature.

- Always use the shape and size of tin specified in each recipe, so as to ensure cooking times are accurate. Line the tin(s) as specified in the recipe, or grease or dust with flour.

- Position a shelf in the centre of the oven, ensuring there is enough room above it to allow room for the cake to rise. Preheat the oven to the required temperature.

- Always weigh and measure ingredients accurately, either with scales or cup measures (although cup measures are never as accurate as weighing the ingredients).

- If melting ingredients in a saucepan, never allow the mixture to boil unless specified.

- Eggs or egg yolks should always be added to a creamed cake mixture one at a time, beating well after each addition.

- If the creamed mixture looks like it may be starting to curdle, sift in a little of the flour alternately with each egg to prevent this.

- When whisking egg whites, ensure the bowl and beaters (or whisk) are clean and dry before you start, or the egg whites won't whisk properly. The egg whites should be at room temperature before whisking.

- A raising agent should always be sifted into the bowl with the flour so that it is evenly dispersed.

- Dry ingredients should always be folded into a whisked egg and sugar mixture with a large metal spoon. Fold lightly and gently from the centre of the bowl outwards, turning the bowl a little with each fold. Fold whisked egg whites into the other ingredients (not the other way round), so as to retain as much aeration as possible.

- Spoon thick cake batters into a tin. Gently pour thinner batters. If necessary, smooth the surface of the batter using a spatula to ensure even cooking and browning.

- Never open the oven door during the first half of cooking time. After the halfway point, if you do need to open the door, open and close it gently.

- If the cooked cake is stuck to the cake tin, run a palette knife gently between the cake and tin before unmoulding.

- Allow the cake to cool a little before inverting it onto a wire rack to cool. So the wire rack does not mark the top of the cake, place another wire rack on the base of the cake and invert the cake onto the second rack so it is right side up.

- If you intend to ice the cake, allow it to cool completely first. If you intend to drizzle it with hot syrup, however, do this while the cake is still hot.

easy sponge cake with strawberries and cream

serves 6

30 g (1 oz) **butter**, melted

60 g (2¹/4 oz/¹/2 cup) **plain (all-purpose) flour**

60 g (2¹/4 oz/¹/2 cup) **cornflour (cornstarch)**

2 teaspoons **cream of tartar**

1 teaspoon **bicarbonate of soda (baking soda)**

4 **eggs**

170 g (6 oz/³/4 cup) **caster (superfine) sugar**

2 tablespoons **hot milk**

300 ml (10¹/2 fl oz) **whipping cream**

1 tablespoon **icing (confectioners') sugar**, plus extra for dusting

2 tablespoons **strawberry jam**

500 g (1 lb 2 oz/3¹/3 cups) **strawberries**, hulled and sliced in half

Preheat the oven to 180°C (350°F/Gas 4). Grease two 20 cm (8 inch) round cake tins with the melted butter and line the bases with baking paper. Dust the sides of the tins with a little flour, shaking out any excess.

Sift the flour, cornflour, cream of tartar and bicarbonate of soda into a bowl, then repeat the sifting twice more.

Whisk the eggs and sugar in a large bowl for 5 minutes, or until pale and thick. Using a large metal spoon, carefully fold in the sifted flour mixture and the hot milk until they are just incorporated; take care not to overmix. Divide the mixture evenly between the two tins, then bake for 18–20 minutes, or until the cakes are golden and have shrunk slightly from the side of the tins. Leave in the tins for 5 minutes, then turn out onto a wire rack to cool.

Combine the cream and icing sugar in a bowl, then whip until soft peaks form. Place one sponge cake on a serving plate and spread with jam. Top with half the cream and half of the sliced strawberries. Cover with the second sponge cake. Spread the remaining cream over the top and top with the remaining strawberries. Dust with icing sugar and serve immediately.

Sponge cake is best eaten on the day it is made. Unfilled sponges will freeze well for up to 1 month, wrapped loosely in plastic wrap.

almond cakes with red wine syrup

makes 6

180 g (6 oz) **unsalted butter**, chopped

230 g (8¹/2 oz/1 cup) **caster (superfine) sugar**

4 **eggs**

125 g (4¹/2 oz/1 cup) **self-raising flour**

35 g (1¹/4 oz/¹/3 cup) **ground almonds**

80 ml (2¹/2 fl oz/¹/3 cup) **milk**

thick (double/heavy) cream, to serve

red wine syrup

350 g (12 oz/1¹/2 cups) **caster (superfine) sugar**

300 ml (10¹/2 fl oz) **red wine**

170 ml (5¹/2 fl oz/²/3 cup) **blackcurrant juice**

Preheat the oven to 200°C (400°F/Gas 6). Lightly grease six 250 ml (9 fl oz/1 cup) capacity kugelhopf tins and dust with flour, shaking out any excess.

Cream the butter and sugar in a bowl using electric beaters until pale and fluffy. Add the eggs one at a time, beating well after each addition. Sift the flour over the mixture and gently stir it in, then add the almonds and milk and stir until just combined. Spoon into the prepared tins and bake for 15–20 minutes, or until a skewer inserted into the centre of a cake comes out clean. Remove from the oven and cool in the tin for 5 minutes, then turn out onto a wire rack.

To make the red wine syrup, put all the ingredients in a small saucepan and stir over a low heat until the sugar has dissolved. Increase the heat to medium and simmer for 10 minutes, or until the liquid is thick and syrupy.

Serve the almond cakes with the warm syrup poured over them and with cream to the side.

108

marble cake

serves 6

1 **vanilla bean** or 1 teaspoon **natural vanilla extract**

185 g (6¹/2 oz) **unsalted butter**, chopped

230 g (8 oz/1 cup) **caster (superfine) sugar**

3 **eggs**

280 g (10 oz/2¹/4 cups) **self-raising flour**

185 ml (6 fl oz/³/4 cup) **milk**

2 tablespoons **unsweetened cocoa powder**

1¹/2 tablespoons **warm milk**, extra

Preheat the oven to 200°C (400°F/Gas 6). Lightly grease a 25 x 11 x 7.5 cm (10 x 4¹/4 x 3 inch) loaf tin and line the base with baking paper.

If using the vanilla bean, split it down the middle and scrape out the seeds. Put the seeds (or vanilla extract) in a bowl with the butter and sugar and, using electric beaters, cream the mixture until pale and fluffy. Add the eggs one at a time, beating well after each addition. Sift the flour, then fold it into the creamed mixture alternately with the milk until combined. Divide the mixture in half and put the second half into another bowl.

Combine the cocoa powder and warm milk in a small bowl and stir until smooth, then add to one half of cake mixture, stirring to combine well. Spoon the two mixtures into the prepared tin in alternate spoonfuls. Using a metal skewer, cut through the mixture four times to create a marble effect. Bake for 50–60 minutes, or until a skewer inserted into the centre of the cake comes out clean. Leave in the tin for 5 minutes before turning out onto a wire rack to cool.

This cake will keep, stored in an airtight container, for 3–4 days. It is also suitable to freeze.

tip Cooling the cake on a wire rack ensures the base of the cake dries out and the cake does not steam in its own heat.

flourless chocolate cake

serves 6–8

150 g (5¹/2 oz) **dark chocolate**, chopped

125 g (4¹/2 oz) **unsalted butter**, chopped

150 g (5¹/2 oz/2/3 cup) **caster
(superfine) sugar**

5 **eggs**, separated

200 g (7 oz/13/4 cups) **ground hazelnuts**

¹/2 teaspoon **baking powder**

40 g (1¹/2 oz/¹/3 cup) **unsweetened
cocoa powder**

1 teaspoon **ground cinnamon**

icing (confectioners') sugar, for dusting

vanilla cream

1 **vanilla bean** or 1 teaspoon
natural vanilla extract

300 ml (10¹/2 fl oz) **whipping cream**

1 tablespoon **caster (superfine) sugar**

Preheat the oven to 170°C (325°F/Gas 3). Lightly grease a 20 cm (8 inch) round cake tin and line the base with baking paper.

Put the chocolate in a heatproof bowl. Sit the bowl over a saucepan of simmering water, stirring frequently until the chocolate has melted. Take care that the base of the bowl doesn't touch the water. Set aside and allow to cool.

Cream the butter and sugar in a bowl using electric beaters until pale and fluffy. Add the egg yolks one at a time, beating well after each addition. Fold in the cooled, melted chocolate. Sift the hazelnuts, baking powder, cocoa powder and cinnamon into a bowl, then fold into the butter mixture.

Whisk the egg whites in a clean, dry bowl until stiff peaks form. Using a large metal spoon, fold the egg whites into the chocolate mixture, working in two batches. Gently spread the mixture into the tin and bake for about 1 hour, or until a skewer inserted into the centre of the cake comes out clean. Cool the cake in the tin.

Meanwhile, make the vanilla cream. If using the vanilla bean, split it down the middle and scrape out the seeds. Beat the cream, vanilla seeds (or vanilla extract) and sugar in small bowl using electric beaters until soft peaks form. Serve the cake dusted with icing sugar and with the vanilla cream.

This cake will keep, stored in an airtight container, for 3–4 days. It is also suitable to freeze.

polenta poundcake with blackberry compote

serves 6–8

150 g (5¹/2 oz) **butter**

230 g (8¹/2 oz/1 cup) **soft brown sugar**

115 g (4 oz/¹/2 cup) **caster (superfine) sugar**

5 **eggs**

185 ml (6 fl oz/³/4 cup) **sour cream**

³/4 teaspoon **almond essence**

1 teaspoon **natural vanilla extract**

155 g (5¹/2 oz/1¹/4 cups) **plain (all-purpose) flour**

1¹/2 teaspoons **baking powder**

150 g (5¹/2 oz/1 cup) **polenta (cornmeal)**

thick (double/heavy) **cream**, to serve

blackberry compote

80 g (2³/4 oz/¹/3 cup) **caster (superfine) sugar**

2 teaspoons **lemon juice**

500 g (1 lb 2 oz) **blackberries**

Preheat the oven to 180°C (350°F/Gas 4). Grease a 24 x 14 cm (9¹/2 x 5¹/2 inch) loaf tin with butter.

Cream the butter, brown sugar and sugar in a large bowl using electric beaters for 2 minutes, or until pale and fluffy. Add the eggs one at a time, beating well after each addition. Reduce the speed to low and mix in the sour cream and almond and vanilla essences.

Sift together the flour, baking powder and a pinch of salt. Add the flour mixture and polenta to the butter mixture and fold in. Pour into the prepared tin. Bake for 50 minutes, or until a skewer inserted into the centre of the cake comes out clean. Leave to cool in the tin for 5 minutes, then unmould the cake by running a knife around the inside edge to loosen. Turn out onto a wire rack to cool.

While the cake is cooking, make the blackberry compote. Combine the sugar, lemon juice and 2 tablespoons water in a saucepan, then stir over medium heat for 3 minutes, or until the sugar dissolves. Add the berries and stir to coat, then bring the mixture to a simmer. Cook over medium–low heat for 5 minutes, stirring occasionally, or until the berries are soft but still holding their shape. Cool to room temperature. Serve at room temperature or chilled.

Cut the cake into thick slices and serve toasted with the compote and cream.

italian christmas cake

serves 18–20

440 g (15¹/2 oz/1¹/4 cups) **honey**

60 ml (2 fl oz/¹/4 cup) **red wine**

235 g (8¹/2 oz/1¹/2 cups) **blanched almonds**, toasted and chopped

450 g (1 lb) **glacé fruit** (choose a mixture of citron, orange, pears, peaches and red glacé cherries), chopped into large chunks

410 g (14¹/2 oz/3¹/3 cups) **plain (all-purpose) flour**

115 g (4 oz/¹/2 cup) **caster (superfine) sugar**

60 g (2¹/4 oz/¹/2 cup) **unsweetened cocoa powder**

80 g (2³/4 oz) **dark chocolate**, finely chopped

¹/4 teaspoon **bicarbonate of soda (baking soda)**

¹/2 teaspoon **ground cinnamon**

¹/2 teaspoon **ground nutmeg**

a large pinch of **ground cloves**

1 teaspoon finely grated **orange zest**

1 teaspoon finely grated **lemon zest**

topping

200 g (7 oz) **glacé orange slices**

30 g (1 oz) **red glacé cherries**

115 g (4 oz/¹/3 cup) **warm honey**

Pour the **honey and red wine** mixture into the dry ingredients.

Decorate the top of the cake with orange slices and **cherries**.

Preheat the oven to 170°C (325°F/Gas 3). Lightly grease a 23 cm (9 inch) round spring-form cake tin and line the base with baking paper. Dust the side of the tin with a little flour, shaking off any excess.

Combine the honey and red wine in a small saucepan and heat, stirring often, over low–medium heat for 2 minutes, or until the honey has just melted and the mixture is smooth.

Combine the almonds, glacé fruit, flour, sugar, cocoa powder, chocolate, bicarbonate of soda, spices and citrus zest in a large bowl and stir to combine well. Pour in the honey mixture, then, using a wooden spoon, stir until a firm dough forms; it may be necessary to use your hands.

Transfer the mixture into the prepared tin and smooth the top. Bake for 60 minutes, or until a skewer inserted into the centre of the cake comes out a little sticky. Using the skewer, pierce the cake all over, decorate with the orange slices and cherries and then spoon over the warm honey. Return the cake to the oven and bake for a further 10 minutes. Allow to cool.

Remove the cake from the tin, leave to cool completely, then wrap in plastic wrap and store for 1–2 days before using. Slice thinly to serve.

This cake will keep, stored in an airtight container, for up to 1 month.

tip Glacé orange slices are available from some delicatessens and health food stores.

white chocolate, almond and cranberry torte

serves 8–10

8 **egg whites**

200 g (7 oz) **caster (superfine) sugar**

250 g (9 oz) good-quality **white chocolate**, chopped

195 g (7 oz/1¼ cups) **whole blanched almonds**, toasted, then chopped

200 g (7 oz/1½ cups) **sweetened dried cranberries**

40 g (1½ oz/⅓ cup) **self-raising flour**

Preheat the oven to 180°C (350°F/Gas 4). Lightly grease a 24 cm (9½ inch) round spring-form cake tin and line the base with baking paper. Dust the side of the tin with a little flour, shaking out any excess.

Whisk the egg whites in a clean, dry bowl until stiff peaks form. Gradually add the sugar, whisking well after each addition. Whisk until the mixture is stiff and glossy and the sugar has dissolved. Put the chocolate, almonds and cranberries into a bowl, add the flour and toss to combine. Gently fold the chocolate mixture into the egg whites. Spread the mixture into the prepared tin and gently tap the base.

Bake for 1 hour, covering the cake with foil halfway through cooking if it begins to brown too quickly. Turn off the oven and leave to cool completely in the oven. Run a knife around the edge of the tin to loosen the torte, then remove it from the tin.

The torte will keep, stored in an airtight container in a cool place, for up to 1 week. It is not suitable to freeze.

tip Sweetened dried cranberries are sometimes labelled as craisins.

carrot and hazelnut cake

serves 8–10

150 g (5¹/2 oz/1 cup) finely grated **carrots**

165 g (5³/4 oz/1¹/2 cups) **ground hazelnuts**

70 g (2¹/2 oz/³/4 cup) dry **breadcrumbs**

a pinch of **ground nutmeg**

6 **eggs**, separated

230 g (8¹/2 oz/1 cup) **caster (superfine) sugar**

2 tablespoons **sweet sherry**

orange glaze

155 g (5¹/2 oz/1¹/4 cups) **icing (confectioners') sugar**, sifted

10 g (¹/4 oz) **unsalted butter**, softened

2–3 tablespoons **orange juice**

Preheat the oven to 180°C (350°F/Gas 4). Lightly grease a 24 cm (9¹/2 inch) round spring-form cake tin and line the base with baking paper. Dust the side of the tin with a little flour, shaking out any excess.

Put the carrots and hazelnuts in a bowl and mix until combined. Add the breadcrumbs and nutmeg and mix until combined, then set aside.

Whisk the egg yolks and sugar in a large bowl for 5 minutes, or until pale and thick. Stir in the sherry, then fold into the carrot mixture.

Whisk the egg whites in a clean, dry bowl until soft peaks form. Gently fold the egg whites, a third at a time, into the carrot mixture. Spoon into the prepared tin and bake for 50 minutes, or until firm to the touch and a skewer inserted into the centre of the cake comes out clean. Leave to cool for 10 minutes, then remove from the tin and transfer to a wire rack to cool completely.

To make the orange glaze, combine the icing sugar and butter in a heatproof bowl, then add just enough orange juice to make a soft, slightly runny glaze. Place the bowl over a saucepan of simmering water and stir for 1–2 minutes, or until the mixture is smooth and glossy. Pour the icing over the top of the cake and smooth over with a flat-bladed knife or palette knife. Allow to set, then serve.

butterless rum fruit cake

serves 12–14

310 g (11 oz/2¹/2 cups) **sultanas (golden raisins)**

250 g (9 oz/2 cups) **raisins**

225 g (8 oz/1¹/2 cups) **currants**

185 ml (6 fl oz/³/4 cup) **vegetable oil**

125 ml (4 fl oz/¹/2 cup) **dark rum**

125 ml (4 fl oz/¹/2 cup) **orange juice**

230 g (8¹/2 oz/1 cup) **soft brown sugar**

2 tablespoons **treacle** or **golden syrup**

¹/2 teaspoon **bicarbonate of soda (baking soda)**

1 tablespoon grated **orange zest**

4 **eggs**, lightly beaten

185 g (6¹/2 oz/1¹/2 cups) **plain (all-purpose) flour**

60 g (2¹/4 oz/¹/2 cup) **self-raising flour**

1 tablespoon **mixed (pumpkin pie) spice**

40 g (1¹/2 oz/¹/4 cup) **blanched whole almonds**

80 g (2³/4 oz/¹/4 cup) **apricot jam**, to glaze

bake it

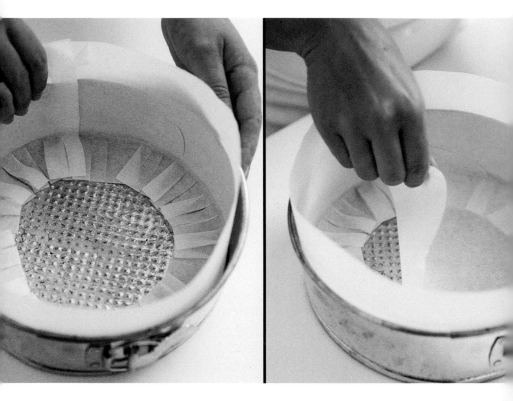

Fit the strip of **baking paper** inside the tin and press the cuts out so they sit flat around **the base**.

Place **the circles** of baking paper in the base of the **tin**.

Preheat the oven to 150°C (300°F/Gas 2). Lightly grease a 20 cm (8 inch) round cake tin. Cut a double layer of baking paper into a strip long enough to fit around the outside of the tin and tall enough to come 5 cm (2 inches) above the edge of the tin. Fold down a cuff about 2 cm (3/4 inch) deep along the length of the strip, along the folded edge. Make cuts along the cuff, cutting up to the fold line, about 1 cm (1/2 inch) apart. Fit the strip around the inside of the tin, with the cuts on the base, pressing the cuts out at right angles so they sit flat around the base. Place the cake tin on a doubled piece of baking paper and draw around the edge. Cut out and sit the paper circles in the base of the tin.

Combine the dried fruit, oil, rum, orange juice, sugar and treacle in a large saucepan and stir over medium heat until the sugar has dissolved. Bring to the boil, reduce the heat and simmer, covered, over low heat for 10 minutes. Remove from the heat and stir in the bicarbonate of soda, then cool to room temperature. Stir in the zest, eggs, sifted flours and mixed spice.

Spread the mixture into the prepared tin and smooth the surface, then arrange the almonds over the top of the cake. Bake for 2 hours 15 minutes, or until a skewer inserted into the centre of the cake comes out clean (the skewer may be slightly sticky if inserted into fruit). Allow to cool in the tin.

Heat the jam in a saucepan over low heat for 3–4 minutes, or until runny. Brush the top of the cake with the jam.

When storing the cake, cover the top with baking paper and then foil to keep it moist. This fruit cake will keep, stored in an airtight container, in a cool place for up to 1 month, or up to 3 months in the freezer.

guinness spice cake

serves 8–10

250 ml (9 fl oz/1 cup) **Guinness**

350 g (12 oz/1 cup) **molasses**

2 teaspoons **baking powder**

3 **eggs**

230 g (8¹/₂ oz/1 cup) **soft brown sugar**

200 ml (7 fl oz) **vegetable oil**

250 g (9 oz/2 cups) **self-raising flour**

2¹/₂ tablespoons **ground ginger**

2 teaspoons **ground cinnamon**

100 g (3¹/₂ oz/¹/₃ cup) **marmalade**

80 g (2³/₄ oz) **candied orange peel quarters**, julienned (optional)

Preheat the oven to 180°C (350°F/Gas 4). Grease a 2.5 litre (87 fl oz/10 cup) kugelhopf tin and lightly dust with flour, shaking out any excess.

Combine the Guinness and molasses in a large saucepan and bring to the boil. Remove from the heat, add the baking powder and allow the foam to subside.

Whisk the eggs and sugar in a large bowl for 1–2 minutes, or until pale and slightly thickened. Add the oil and whisk to combine, then add to the beer mixture. Sift the flour and spices into a large bowl. Gradually whisk in the beer mixture until combined. Pour into the prepared tin and bake for 1 hour, or until firm to the touch and a skewer inserted into the centre of the cake comes out clean. Cool in the tin for 20 minutes, then turn out onto a wire rack.

Heat the marmalade in a saucepan over low heat for 3–4 minutes, or until runny. Strain, then brush the top of the cake with some of the marmalade. Arrange the candied orange peel strips, if using, on top and brush with the remaining marmalade.

This cake will keep, stored in an airtight container, for up to 7 days, or frozen for up to 3 months.

tip Candied orange peel is available in thick pieces (about the size of a quarter of an orange) from specialist food stores and delicatessens.

pistachio friends

makes 10

165 g (5³/4 oz/1¹/3 cups) **icing (confectioners') sugar**, plus extra for dusting

40 g (1¹/2 oz/¹/3 cup) **plain (all-purpose) flour**

125 g (4¹/2 oz/1 cup) ground **pistachio nuts** (see tip, page 327)

160 g (5³/4 oz) **unsalted butter**, melted

5 **egg whites**, lightly beaten

¹/2 teaspoon **natural vanilla extract**

55 g (2 oz/¹/4 cup) **caster (superfine) sugar**

35 g (1¹/4 oz/¹/4 cup) chopped **pistachio nuts**

Preheat the oven to 190°C (375°F/Gas 5). Lightly grease ten 125 ml (4 fl oz/¹/2 cup) friand tins.

Sift the icing sugar and flour into a bowl. Add the ground pistachios, butter, egg whites and vanilla and stir with a metal spoon until just combined.

Spoon the mixture into the prepared tins, place on a baking tray and bake for 15–20 minutes, or until a skewer inserted into the centre of a friand comes out clean. Leave in the tins for 5 minutes, then turn out onto a wire rack to cool.

Meanwhile, put the sugar and 60 ml (2 fl oz/¹/4 cup) water in a small saucepan and stir over low heat until the sugar has dissolved. Increase the heat, then boil for 4 minutes, or until thick and syrupy. Remove from the heat and stir in the chopped pistachios, then, working quickly, spoon the mixture over the tops of the friands. Dust with icing sugar and serve.

Friands will keep, stored in an airtight container, for up to 4 days, or frozen for up to 3 months.

tip Friand tins can be purchased from kitchenware shops. Alternatively, you can bake the friands in a 12-hole standard muffin tin.

rice flour and madeira friands

makes 18

250 g (9 oz) **unsalted butter**, softened

350 g (12 oz/1½ cups) **caster (superfine) sugar**

8 **eggs**

1 teaspoon finely grated **orange zest**

80 g (2¾ oz/¾ cup) **ground almonds**

300 g (10½ oz/1¾ cups) **rice flour**, sifted

60 ml (2 fl oz/¼ cup) **madeira**

80 g (2¾ oz/½ cup) chopped **blanched almonds**

icing (confectioners') sugar, for dusting

whipped cream and **berries**, to serve

Preheat the oven to 170°C (325°F/Gas 3). Grease eighteen 125 ml (4 fl oz/½ cup) friand tins.

Cream the butter and sugar in a bowl using electric beaters until pale and fluffy. Add the eggs one at a time, beating well after each addition, then add the orange zest and continue to beat for 5 minutes. Combine the ground almonds and rice flour and fold into the butter mixture, in three stages, alternately with the madeira, until just combined.

Spoon the mixture into the prepared tins and sprinkle over the almonds. Bake for 25–30 minutes, or until golden and a skewer inserted into the centre of a friand comes out clean. Leave in the tins for 5 minutes, then turn out onto a wire rack to cool. Dust with icing sugar and serve with whipped cream and berries.

The friands will keep, stored in an airtight container, for up to 4 days, or frozen for up to 3 months.

tip If madeira is unavailable, substitute sweet sherry.

polenta fruit cake

serves 6–8

150 g (5¹/2 oz/1 cup) **polenta (cornmeal)**

60 g (2¹/4 oz) **unsalted butter**, chopped

115 g (4 oz/¹/2 cup) **caster (superfine) sugar**

150 g (5¹/2 oz) **pitted dates**, chopped

95 g (3¹/4 oz/¹/2 cup) chopped **dried apricots**

a pinch of **nutmeg**

1¹/2 teaspoons finely grated **lemon zest**

2 **eggs**, lightly beaten

125 g (4¹/2 oz/1 cup) **plain (all-purpose) flour**, sifted

55 g (2 oz/¹/3 cup) **pine nuts**

icing (confectioners') sugar, for dusting

Preheat the oven to 180°C (350°F/Gas 4). Grease a 21 x 11 cm (8¹/4 x 4¹/4 inch) loaf tin and line the base with baking paper.

Bring 500 ml (17 fl oz/2 cups) water to the boil in a large saucepan. Gradually add the polenta and a pinch of salt, stirring constantly. Reduce the heat to medium, add the butter and continue to stir for 1–2 minutes, or until the mixture thickens and comes away from the side of the pan. Remove from the heat, allow to cool slightly, then add all the remaining ingredients, except the pine nuts.

Spoon the mixture into the prepared tin, smoothing the surface with the back of a wet spoon. Sprinkle the pine nuts over the top and press gently onto the top of the cake. Bake for 40–45 minutes, or until firm and a skewer inserted into the centre of the cake comes out clean. Leave in the tin for 10 minutes, then turn out onto a wire rack to cool. Dust with icing sugar and serve.

Polenta fruit cake will keep, stored in an airtight container, for up to 3 days.

chocolate chestnut roulade

serves 6–8

60 g (2¹/4 oz) **dark chocolate**, chopped

4 **eggs**

115 g (4 oz/¹/2 cup) **caster (superfine) sugar**

100 g (3¹/3 oz) **tinned sweetened chestnut purée**

60 g (2¹/4 oz/¹/2 cup) **self-raising flour**, sifted

2 tablespoons **hot water**

unsweetened cocoa powder, for dusting

chestnut cream

150 g (5¹/2 oz) **tinned sweetened chestnut purée**

300 ml (10¹/2 fl oz) **thick (double/heavy) cream**

1 tablespoon **dark rum**

Starting from the long side, carefully **roll up the cake**, enclosing the baking paper inside the roll.

Spread **the cream** over the cooled cake, then roll it up again, using the **paper** to guide you.

Preheat the oven to 180°C (350°F/Gas 4). Lightly grease a 25 x 30 cm (10 x 12 inch) shallow Swiss roll tin (jelly roll tin) and line the base with baking paper.

Put the chocolate in a heatproof bowl. Sit the bowl over a saucepan of simmering water, stirring frequently until the chocolate has melted. Take care that the base of the bowl doesn't touch the water. Allow to cool.

Whisk the eggs and sugar in a large bowl for 5 minutes, or until pale and very thick. Beat in the chestnut purée and chocolate, then fold in the flour and water. Gently spread the mixture into the prepared tin and bake for 20 minutes, or until just cooked and springy to the touch (do not overcook or the cake will crack when it is rolled).

Put a tea towel (dish towel) on the work surface, cover with a sheet of baking paper and sprinkle the paper lightly with cocoa powder. Turn the cake out onto the paper, then carefully remove the baking paper from the base of the cake. Trim the edges to neaten. Using the tea towel as a guide, carefully roll the cake up from the long side, rolling the paper inside the roll. Put the rolled cake on a wire rack and leave to cool for 10 minutes, then carefully unroll the cake and cool completely.

To make the chestnut cream, combine the purée, cream and rum in a small bowl, then beat until just thick. Spread the cake with the chestnut cream, then carefully reroll, using the paper to guide you. Place the roulade seam side down and dust the top lightly with cocoa powder.

This roulade is best eaten on the day it is made.

blueberry semolina cakes

makes 12

30 g (1 oz/1/4 cup) **self-raising flour**

40 g (11/2 oz/1/3 cup) **semolina**

230 g (8 oz/1 cup) **caster (superfine) sugar**

25 g (1 oz/1/4 cup) **ground almonds**

1/2 teaspoon finely grated **lemon zest**

4 **egg whites**, lightly beaten

125 g (41/2 oz) **unsalted butter**, melted

80 g (23/4 oz/1/2 cup) **blueberries**

45 g (11/2 oz/1/2 cup) **flaked almonds**

icing (confectioners') sugar, for dusting

Preheat the oven to 170°C (325°F/Gas 3). Line a 12-hole standard muffin tin with paper cases.

Sift the flour and semolina into a large bowl and add the sugar, ground almonds and lemon zest and stir to combine. Add the egg whites and, using electric beaters, beat until the ingredients are combined. Pour in the melted butter and continue to beat until smooth and well combined. Add the blueberries and fold in to just combine, then spoon the batter into the paper cases.

Sprinkle the flaked almonds over the cakes and bake for 30 minutes, or until a skewer inserted into the centre of a cake comes out clean. Turn out onto a wire rack to cool. Dust with icing sugar to serve.

The blueberry cakes are best served on the day they are made.

yoghurt banana cakes with honey icing

makes 2 cakes, each serving 8

180 g (6 oz) **unsalted butter**, softened

90 g (3¼ oz/¼ cup) **honey**

230 g (8 oz/1 cup) **caster (superfine) sugar**

1½ teaspoons **natural vanilla extract**

3 **eggs**

360 g (12¾ oz/1½ cups) **mashed ripe banana** — about 4 bananas

185 g (6½ oz/¾ cup) **plain yoghurt**

½ teaspoon **bicarbonate of soda (baking soda)**

375 g (13 oz/3 cups) **self-raising flour**, sifted

honey icing

125 g (4½ oz) **unsalted butter**

3 tablespoons **honey**

125 g (4½ oz/1 cup) **icing (confectioners') sugar**

1 tablespoon **milk**

Preheat the oven to 180°C (350°F/Gas 4). Lightly grease two 15 cm (6 inch) round cake tins and line the bases with baking paper.

Cream the butter, honey, sugar and vanilla in a bowl using electric beaters until pale and fluffy. Add the eggs one at a time, beating well after each addition, then beat in the banana.

Combine the yoghurt and bicarbonate of soda in a small bowl. Fold the flour alternately with the yoghurt into the banana mixture. Divide the mixture evenly between the tins, smoothing the tops. Bake for 50–60 minutes, or until a skewer inserted into the centre of a cake comes out clean. Cool in the tins for 5 minutes, then turn out onto a wire rack.

To make the honey icing, cream the butter and honey in a small bowl using electric beaters until pale and fluffy. Gradually add the icing sugar alternately with the milk, beating well until the mixture is very pale. When the cakes are cold, divide the honey icing between the tops, spreading the icing to form rough peaks.

These cakes will keep, stored in an airtight container, for up to 4 days. Un-iced cakes can be frozen for up to 3 months.

bake it

coffee syrup cakes

makes 6

1¹/2 tablespoons **instant coffee
 granules**
90 g (3¹/4 oz/¹/3 cup) **sour cream**
125 g (4¹/2 oz) **unsalted butter**
165 g (5³/4 oz/³/4 cup) firmly packed
 soft brown sugar
2 **eggs**
155 g (5¹/2 oz/1¹/4 cups) **self-raising
 flour**, sifted

coffee syrup
2 teaspoons **instant coffee granules**
165 g (5³/4 oz/³/4 cup) firmly packed
 soft brown sugar

Preheat the oven to 180°C (350°F/Gas 4). Lightly grease six mini 250 ml (9 fl oz/ 1 cup) rectangular tins, then lightly dust with flour, shaking out any excess.

Dissolve the coffee in 2 tablespoons boiling water in a bowl. Allow to cool, then add the sour cream and stir to combine well.

Cream the butter and sugar in a bowl using electric beaters until pale and fluffy. Add the eggs one at a time, beating well after each addition. Fold in the flour alternately with the sour cream mixture, then divide the mixture between the prepared tins and smooth the tops. Bake for about 25 minutes, or until a skewer inserted into the centre of a cake comes out clean.

To make the coffee syrup, combine the coffee, sugar and 170 ml (5¹/2 fl oz/²/3 cup) water in a small saucepan and stir over medium heat until the sugar has dissolved. Bring to the boil, then remove from the heat. Spoon the hot coffee syrup over the hot cakes in the tin and allow to cool before turning out onto a wire rack.

Coffee cakes will keep, stored in an airtight container, for 3–4 days, or up to 3 months in the freezer.

olive oil and sweet wine cake

serves 6–8

3 **eggs**

170 g (6 oz/3/4 cup) **caster (superfine) sugar**

2 teaspoons finely grated **orange zest**

2 teaspoons finely grated **lemon zest**

2 teaspoons finely grated **lime zest**

60 ml (2 fl oz/1/4 cup) **extra virgin olive oil**

60 ml (2 fl oz/1/4 cup) **olive oil**

185 g (61/2 oz/11/2 cups) **self-raising flour**, sifted

125 ml (4 fl oz/1/2 cup) **late-harvest white wine**

icing (confectioners') sugar, for dusting

Preheat the oven to 180°C (350°F/Gas 4). Grease a deep 20 cm (8 inch) round cake tin and line the base with baking paper. Dust the side of the tin with a little flour, shaking out any excess.

Whisk the eggs and sugar in a large bowl for 3–5 minutes, or until pale and thick. Add the orange, lemon and lime zests and both the oils and beat until combined. Fold in the flour alternately with the wine until combined.

Pour into the prepared tin and bake for 40–45 minutes, or until a skewer inserted into the centre of the cake comes out clean. Leave to cool in the tin for 10 minutes, then turn out onto a wire rack. Dust with icing sugar to serve.

This cake will keep, stored in an airtight container, for 4 days, or frozen for up to 3 months.

low-fat chocolate cake

serves 12

3 **eggs**

185 g (61/2 oz/1 cup) lightly packed **soft brown sugar**

40 g (11/2 oz) **unsalted butter**, melted

170 ml (51/2 fl oz/2/3 cup) ready-made **apple sauce**

60 ml (2 fl oz/1/4 cup) **low-fat milk**

85 g (3 oz/2/3 cup) **unsweetened cocoa powder**

185 g (61/2 oz/11/2 cups) **self-raising flour**

chocolate icing

125 g (41/2 oz/1 cup) **icing (confectioners') sugar**, sifted

2 tablespoons **unsweetened cocoa powder**

1–2 tablespoons **low-fat milk**

Preheat the oven to 180°C (350°F/Gas 4). Brush a 20 cm (8 inch) kugelhopf tin with melted butter, dust lightly with flour and shake out any excess.

Whisk the eggs and sugar in a bowl for 5 minutes, or until pale and thick. Combine the butter, apple sauce and milk in a small bowl, stirring to mix well, then fold into the egg mixture. Sift the cocoa powder and flour together into a bowl, then fold into the egg mixture.

Pour the mixture into the tin and bake for 35–40 minutes, or until a skewer inserted into the centre of the cake comes out clean. Leave the cake to cool in the tin for 5 minutes, then turn out onto a wire rack to cool completely.

To make the chocolate icing, combine the icing sugar and cocoa powder in a bowl, then stir in enough milk to form a thick paste. Stand the bowl over a saucepan of simmering water, stirring until the icing is smooth, then remove from the heat. Spread the icing over the cake and leave to set.

This chocolate cake is best eaten on the day it is made.

lemon and honey ricotta cake

serves 10–12

1 kg (2 lb 4 oz/4 cups) **fresh ricotta cheese** (see tip)

175 g (6 oz/1/2 cup) **honey**

1 1/2 teaspoons **natural vanilla extract**

60 ml (2 fl oz/1/4 cup) **lemon juice**

finely grated **zest** from 2 **lemons**

1/2 teaspoon **ground cinnamon**

4 **eggs**, lightly beaten

35 g (1 1/4 oz/1/4 cup) **plain (all-purpose) flour**

poached nectarines or **peaches**, to serve (optional)

Preheat the oven to 170°C (325°F/Gas 3). Lightly grease and flour an 18 cm (7 inch) round spring-form cake tin.

Drain the ricotta if necessary, then process in a food processor until smooth. Add the honey, vanilla, lemon juice, zest, cinnamon and eggs and process until well combined. Add the flour and pulse until just combined and the mixture is smooth.

Spoon the mixture into the prepared tin and bake for 1 hour, or until light golden and still slightly soft in the middle. Turn the oven off, open the door slightly and cool the cake in the oven. Put in the refrigerator to chill, then remove the cake from the tin. Serve at room temperature with poached fruit such as peaches or nectarines, if desired.

tip Buy fresh ricotta cheese sold in a large block at the delicatessen. It has a much better texture than the ricotta cheese sold in tubs.

151

ginger cakes with chocolate centres

makes 12

100 g (3¹/2 oz) **unsalted butter**, softened

125 g (4¹/2 oz/2/3 cup) lightly packed **soft brown sugar**

115 g (4 oz/¹/3 cup) **treacle** or **dark corn syrup**

2 **eggs**

125 g (4¹/2 oz/1 cup) **self-raising flour**

85 g (3 oz/2/3 cup) **plain (all-purpose) flour**

2 teaspoons **ground cinnamon**

1 tablespoon **ground ginger**

60 ml (2 fl oz/¹/4 cup) **buttermilk**

ginger ganache

100 g (3¹/2 oz) good-quality **dark chocolate**, chopped

60 ml (2 fl oz/¹/4 cup) **pouring cream**

1 tablespoon finely chopped **glacé ginger**

Divide the ganache into **twelve** equal portions and roll each into **a ball**.

Divide three-quarters of the **mixture** between the cases. Top with a ganache ball and cover **with the** remaining mixture.

Preheat the oven to 180°C (350°F/Gas 4). Line a 12-hole standard muffin tin with paper cases.

To make the ginger ganache, put the chocolate in a small heatproof bowl. Heat the cream until almost boiling, then pour over the chocolate and stir until it has melted and the mixture is smooth. Stir in the ginger. Cool to room temperature, then chill in the refrigerator until firm. Divide the mixture into 12 equal portions and roll each into a ball. Freeze until required.

Cream the butter, sugar and treacle in a small bowl using electric beaters until pale and fluffy. Add the eggs one at a time, beating well after each addition. Transfer to a large bowl. Sift the flours and spices into a bowl, then fold into the butter mixture alternately with the buttermilk.

Divide three-quarters of the mixture between the paper cases. Top each with a ball of frozen ginger ganache, then spread the remaining mixture over the top of the ganache to cover. Bake for 25–30 minutes, or until deep golden (the cakes cannot be tested with a skewer as the centres will be molten). Leave to cool for 5 minutes, then remove from the muffin holes. Remove the paper cases and serve warm.

These ginger cakes will keep, stored in an airtight container, for up to 4 days, or up to 3 months in the freezer. Reheat to serve.

tip Treacle is a blend of concentrated refinery syrups and extract molasses. It is used in baking to give a distinctive colour and flavour. Golden syrup can be substituted but has a milder flavour.

vanilla and cream cheese cakes

makes 12

60 g (2¹/4 oz) **unsalted butter**, softened

115 g (4 oz/¹/2 cup) **caster (superfine) sugar**

1 teaspoon finely grated **lemon zest**

1 **egg**

1 **egg yolk**

60 g (2¹/4 oz/¹/2 cup) **plain (all-purpose) flour**

1 tablespoon **self-raising flour**

2 tablespoons **sour cream**

cheesecake topping

250 g (9 oz) **cream cheese**, softened

115 g (4 oz/¹/2 cup) **caster (superfine) sugar**

2 **eggs**

160 g (5³/4 oz/²/3 cup) **sour cream**

1 **vanilla bean** or 1 teaspoon **natural vanilla extract**

2 tablespoons **pine nuts**

Preheat the oven to 180°C (350°F/Gas 4). Lightly grease 12 x 125 ml (4 fl oz/¹/2 cup) friand tins and line the bases with baking paper. Dust the sides of the tins with a little flour, shaking off any excess.

Cream the butter, sugar and zest in a bowl using electric beaters until pale and fluffy. Add the egg, then the egg yolk, beating well after each addition. Sift the flours into a bowl, then gently stir into the butter mixture alternately with the sour cream.

Divide the mixture between the friand tins. Bake for 15 minutes, or until a skewer inserted into the centre of a cake comes out clean. Remove from the oven and allow to cool. Reduce the oven to 160°C (315°F/Gas 2–3).

To make the cheesecake topping, beat the cream cheese and sugar in a small bowl until pale and fluffy. Add the eggs one at a time, beating well after each addition, then beat in the sour cream. If using the vanilla bean, split it down the middle and scrape out the seeds. Add the seeds (or vanilla extract) to the cheese mixture, mixing well. Spoon the topping evenly over the cooled cakes and sprinkle with the pine nuts.

Return to the oven and bake for 15 minutes, or until the topping is just set. Remove from the oven, leave to cool slightly, then run a knife around the edge of the cakes to loosen them. Turn out onto a wire rack and allow to cool.

The cakes will keep, stored in an airtight container in the refrigerator, for 3 days.

little jam-filled cakes

makes 12

280 g (10 oz/2¹/4 cups) **self-raising flour**
170 g (6 oz/³/4 cup) **caster (superfine) sugar**
250 ml (9 fl oz/1 cup) **milk**
2 **eggs**, lightly beaten
¹/2 teaspoon **natural vanilla extract**
75 g (2¹/2 oz) **unsalted butter**, melted
80 g (2³/4 oz/¹/4 cup) **strawberry jam**
12 small **strawberries**, hulled
icing (confectioners') sugar, for dusting

Preheat the oven to 200°C (400°F/Gas 6). Grease a 12-hole standard muffin tin.

Sift the flour into a bowl, add the sugar and stir to combine. Make a well in the centre. Put the milk, eggs, vanilla and butter in a bowl, whisking to combine. Pour into the well and, using a metal spoon, gradually fold the milk mixture into the flour mixture until just combined. Divide three-quarters of the cake batter between the muffin holes. Top each with 1 teaspoon of the jam and cover with the remaining cake batter. Gently press a strawberry into the centre.

Bake for 20 minutes, or until light golden. Cool in the tin for 5 minutes, then turn out onto a wire rack to cool completely. Dust with icing sugar to serve.

The cakes are best served on the day they are made.

biscuits

about biscuits

The making of biscuits, like that of cakes, can be traced back to ancient Egypt, although they barely resembled the biscuits we bake today. The actual word 'biscuit' comes from the two French words, *bis* (twice) and *cuit* (cooked), referring to small discs of twice-cooked dough, usually savoury, that were given to sailors and soldiers during their long sojourns because they kept so well.

From the 17th century onwards, biscuits were regularly sweetened with sugar and became commonplace in more prosperous households, where home baking had become popular. During this time, the introduction of bakers' guilds meant recipes were standardized and recorded. As the use of domestic ovens increased, biscuit-making soon became very much part of the home baker's repertoire. Today there are thousands of different types of commercially produced biscuits — all readily available and relatively inexpensive — but there is nothing better than home-cooked biscuits, fresh from the oven.

what's in a name?

Biscuits or cookies? The word 'cookie' is often used instead of biscuit, especially in America, and is derived from the Dutch *koekje*, meaning 'little cake'. In England, they're called biscuits, in America it's a cookie, and in Australia it can be either. Although there are historical references to a cookie being a softer, slightly larger style of biscuit, today the two words are more or less interchangeable and both are used universally.

biscuits today

We bake biscuits for birthdays, for festive occasions, for an afternoon snack, and sometimes just for the love of baking. Biscuit-making shares many similarities with both cake- and pastry-making, but is somehow less daunting. They all share the same basic ingredients — flour, fat and liquid (often enriched with eggs and sugar) and similar preparation techniques. Biscuits, like cakes, can be creamed, whisked and melted-in; or, like pastry, biscuit dough can be rolled out and cutters used to stamp out shapes. Shapes and sizes vary too. Some are stamped out, others are formed into blocks or logs and refrigerated until firm enough to slice and bake. Some doughs are shaped into small balls and flattened into rounds, while others are shaped and moulded. Softer doughs are dropped a spoonful at a time onto a baking tray or can be piped directly onto the tray, where they spread slightly before setting.

In biscuit-making, the recipe needs to be followed exactly, so make sure you follow the method and weigh the ingredients carefully. Even so, biscuits aren't supposed to be perfect — they just need to be fun to make and delicious to eat.

essential ingredients

flour

plain (all-purpose) flour: Most often used in biscuit-making. It is a combination of soft and hard wheat varieties, which means that it contains sufficient gluten to enable the dough to stretch, but not so much that the biscuit becomes tough. Overworking the dough can also produce a tough biscuit. Wholemeal (whole-wheat) flour can be used in part with plain flour.

self-raising flour: This is plain flour that already has baking powder (and salt) added to it.

fat

butter: Butter gives the best flavour to biscuits. It tenderizes and shortens the dough. Unsalted butter is best used for sweet biscuits, and salted butter can be used for savoury ones.

Copha (white vegetable shortening): Used in combination with butter or on its own. It literally 'shortens' the texture of a biscuit and prevents it from spreading so much in the oven.

sweeteners

Sweeteners not only make biscuits sweet but they also give them crispness and colour as the sugar that they contain caramelizes in the oven. All natural sweeteners can be used, but they give a slightly different result. Artificial sweeteners are not suitable for use in baking.

caster (superfine) sugar and granulated sugar: Used most frequently in biscuits and gives them the most crispness.

icing (confectioners') sugar: Granulated sugar that has been processed into a fine powder. As it has a little cornflour added to it, it cannot be substituted for caster sugar. It gives a lighter, softer texture to biscuits.

soft brown sugar: Adds a delicate caramel flavour and deeper colour to a biscuit. It tends to give a slightly more chewy result.

golden (or dark corn) syrup: This is a thick liquid sugar, which keeps the moisture in dough. It keeps biscuits fresh for longer. It is interchangeable with dark treacle, although the latter has a deeper colour.

eggs

Eggs add moisture, richness and structure to a biscuit. When beaten in, they also help leaven the dough. Whole eggs, egg yolks or whites can all be used. Egg yolks bind, add richness and tenderize, whilst the egg whites aerate and add strength and stability to a biscuit.

leaveners

Baking powder, bicarbonate of soda (baking soda) and egg whites all provide varying degrees of leavening, as well as giving texture and flavour to biscuits. Leaveners need to be stored correctly to maintain their freshness. Always read the packet instructions and store as directed.

optional additions

cornflour (cornstarch) and rice flour: Cornflour is added in part to biscuit dough to make it more tender. Rice flour acts in the same way as cornflour and tenderizes the biscuit dough.

polenta (cornmeal): Gives a wonderfully nutty flavour and crumbly texture to biscuits.

oatmeal and bran: These add interesting texture and flavour to biscuits and can be used in both sweet and savoury doughs.

other flavourings: Because many basic biscuit mixtures are similar, they rely on a multitude of additional flavours for variety: dried fruits, ground and chopped nuts, chunks of chocolate, spices, citrus peel and juice. Savoury biscuits are flavoured with herbs, spices, seeds, nuts and cheese.

hints and tips

- An electric hand mixer is very useful for whisking and creaming.

- Some recipes can be made using a food processor, however biscuit dough should not be overworked or an excess of gluten will develop, resulting in a tough biscuit. Only use a processor to rub the fat into the flour. When the liquid is added, pulse briefly until the mixture just comes together, then turn out onto a work surface to bring together into a smooth, soft ball, without kneading. Then cut or shape as directed.

- Always weigh and measure ingredients accurately.

- Make sure your ingredients are at the right temperature. Chilled butter means butter straight out of the refrigerator. Softened butter means butter returned to room temperature — this takes about 45 minutes. Eggs also need to be at room temperature. Remove them from the refrigerator about 45 minutes before using.

- Prepare baking trays as specified. Not all recipes require the tray to be greased or lined.

- Always preheat the oven to the required temperature and test with an oven thermometer.

- Make sure the oven shelves are set at an equal distance apart if cooking more than one tray at a time.

- Biscuits spread during baking, some more than others. Most average sized baking trays fit three rows of five biscuits, with the biscuit mixture spaced about 5 cm (2 inches) apart.

- Lightly flour the work surface and rolling pin before and during rolling if the dough starts to stick. Do not use excessive amounts of flour or it can affect the biscuit.

- If using a pastry cutter to stamp out shapes, dip the cutting edge into a little extra flour from time to time to prevent sticking.

- Biscuits can be baked on two trays at the same time, but often the tray underneath will require a longer cooking time. If you have time, cook the biscuits in batches. Alternatively, switch the trays halfway through cooking time.

- Always place biscuit dough onto a cold baking tray. If baking in batches, allow the tray to cool before adding the next batch.

- Always bake for the minimum time given and check for doneness. Cook for only 2 minutes more and then retest (biscuits can be underdone one minute and then burnt the next).

- Always cool biscuits on a wire cooling rack or they can become soggy. Allow biscuits to cool completely before icing or filling.

- Some biscuit recipes call for nuts, whether whole, chopped or ground. Nuts are often toasted before being ground. To toast nuts, put them in a single layer on a baking tray and bake in a preheated 180°C (350°F/ Gas 4) oven for 5–10 minutes, depending on the type of nut or whether they are ground or whole. Always time this or keep a good check on them, as nuts are easy to burn.

mandarin whirls

makes 18 'sandwiches'

350 g (12 oz) **unsalted butter,**
   softened

60 g (2¼ oz/½ cup) **icing**
   (confectioners') sugar

grated **zest** from 2 **mandarins**

250 g (9 oz/2 cups) **plain (all-purpose)**
   flour

60 g (2¼ oz/½ cup) **cornflour**
   (cornstarch)

icing

120 g (4¼ oz) **unsalted butter,**
   softened

250 g (9 oz/2 cups) **icing**
   (confectioners') sugar

2 tablespoons freshly squeezed
   mandarin juice

Preheat the oven to 180°C (350°F/Gas 4). Line two baking trays with baking paper.

Cream the butter, icing sugar and zest in a bowl using electric beaters until pale and fluffy. Sift the flour and cornflour into the bowl, then stir with a wooden spoon until a soft dough forms.

Transfer the mixture to a piping bag fitted with a 4 cm (1½ inch) star nozzle and pipe thirty-six 4 cm (1½ inch) rounds, spacing them well apart, on the baking trays. Bake for 12–15 minutes, or until lightly golden on the edges. Cool on the trays for 5 minutes, then transfer to a wire rack to cool completely.

To make the icing, cream the butter, icing sugar and mandarin juice in a bowl using electric beaters until pale and soft. Use the icing to sandwich the whirls together.

Filled biscuits are best served on the day they are made. Unfilled biscuits will keep, stored in an airtight container, for up to 1 week, or frozen for up to 3 months.

plum and caraway biscuits

makes 24

80 g (2³/4 oz) **butter**, softened

60 g (2¹/4 oz) **cream cheese**, chopped

115 g (4 oz/¹/2 cup) **caster (superfine) sugar**

1 teaspoon **natural vanilla extract**

2 **egg yolks**

1¹/2 teaspoons **caraway seeds**

150 g (5¹/2 oz/1¹/4 cups) **plain (all-purpose) flour**

plum jam

icing (confectioners') sugar, for dusting

Cream the butter, cream cheese and sugar in a bowl using electric beaters until pale and fluffy. Add the vanilla and 1 egg yolk and beat to combine well. Add the caraway seeds and flour and stir until a dough forms. Turn the dough out onto a lightly floured work surface, form into a flat rectangle, then cover with plastic wrap and refrigerate for 2 hours, or until firm.

Preheat the oven to 180°C (350°F/Gas 4). Lightly grease two baking trays. Combine the remaining egg yolk with 2 teaspoons water and stir to combine well.

Cut the dough in half, then roll out each half on a lightly floured work surface to form an 18 x 24 cm (7 x 9¹/2 inch) rectangle. Using a lightly floured sharp knife, cut the dough into 6 cm (2¹/2 inch) squares. Place a scant teaspoon of jam diagonally across the centre of each square, then brush all four corners of the square with the egg mixture. Take one corner and fold it into the centre. Take the opposite corner and fold it into the centre, overlapping the first corner slightly, to partially enclose the jam.

Brush the tops of the biscuits with the egg mixture, then place them, seam side up, on the baking trays. Bake for 10–12 minutes, or until light golden, swapping the position of the trays halfway through cooking. Cool on the trays for 5 minutes, then transfer to a wire rack to cool completely. Dust with icing sugar before serving.

The biscuits will keep, stored in an airtight container, for up to 1 week.

classic shortbread

makes 16 wedges

225 g (8 oz) **unsalted butter**

115 g (4 oz/1/2 cup) **caster (superfine) sugar**, plus extra for dusting

225 g (8 oz/1 3/4 cups) **plain (all-purpose) flour**

115 g (4 oz/2/3 cup) **rice flour**

Preheat the oven to 190°C (375°F/Gas 5). Lightly grease two baking trays.

Cream the butter and sugar in a bowl using electric beaters until pale and fluffy. Sift in the flour, rice flour and a pinch of salt and, using a wooden spoon, stir into the creamed mixture until it resembles fine breadcrumbs. Transfer to a lightly floured work surface and knead gently to form a soft dough. Cover with plastic wrap and refrigerate for 30 minutes.

Divide the dough in half and roll out one half on a lightly floured work surface to form a 20 cm (8 inch) round. Carefully transfer to a prepared tray. Using a sharp knife, score the surface of the dough into eight equal wedges, prick the surface lightly with a fork and, using your fingers, press the edges to form a fluted effect. Repeat this process using the remaining dough to make a second round. Lightly dust the shortbreads with the extra sugar.

Bake for 18–20 minutes, or until the shortbreads are light golden. Remove from the oven and while still hot, follow the score marks and cut into wedges. Cool on the baking tray for 5 minutes, then transfer to a wire rack.

The shortbread will keep, stored in an airtight container, for up to 1 week.

tip Shortbread can be made with plain flour alone; however, the addition of rice flour produces a lighter result.

gingerbread

makes about 40 (depending on size of cutters)

350 g (12 oz) **plain (all-purpose) flour**
2 teaspoons **baking powder**
2 teaspoons **ground ginger**
100 g (3¹/2 oz) chilled **unsalted butter,** diced
175 g (6 oz/³/4 cup) **soft brown sugar**
1 **egg,** beaten
115 g (4 oz/¹/3 cup) **dark treacle**
silver balls (optional)

icing glaze

1 **egg white**
3 teaspoons **lemon juice**
155 g (5¹/2 oz/1¹/4 cups) **icing (confectioners') sugar**

royal icing

1 **egg white**
200 g (7 oz) **icing (confectioners') sugar**

Pour in the **egg** and treacle and stir to form a soft dough.

Cut out **shapes** from the dough using an assortment of **biscuit cutters**.

Preheat the oven to 190°C (375°F/Gas 5). Lightly grease two baking trays.

Sift the flour, baking powder, ground ginger and a pinch of salt into a bowl. Rub in the butter until the mixture resembles fine breadcrumbs, then stir in the sugar. Make a well in the centre, add the egg and treacle and, using a wooden spoon, stir until a soft dough forms. Transfer to a clean surface and knead until smooth.

Divide the dough in half and roll out on a lightly floured work surface until 5 mm (1/4 inch) thick. Using various-shaped cutters (hearts, stars or flowers), cut into desired shapes, then transfer to the prepared trays. Bake in batches for 8 minutes, or until the biscuits are light brown. Cool on the trays for 2–3 minutes, then transfer to a wire rack to cool completely. (If using the biscuits as hanging decorations, use a skewer to make a small hole in each one while still hot.)

To make the glaze, whisk the egg white and lemon juice together until foamy, then whisk in the icing sugar to form a smooth, thin icing. Cover the surface with plastic wrap until needed.

To make the royal icing, lightly whisk the egg white until just foamy, then gradually whisk in enough icing sugar to form a soft icing. Cover the surface with plastic wrap until needed.

Brush a thin layer of glaze over some of the biscuits and leave to set. Using an icing bag (or see tip, below) filled with royal icing, decorate the biscuits as shown in the photograph, or as desired.

Store glazed gingerbread for up to 3 days in an airtight container.

tip To make a paper icing bag, cut a piece of baking paper into a 19 cm (71/2 inch) square and then cut in half diagonally to form two triangles. Hold the triangle, with the longest side away from you, and curl the left hand point over and in towards the centre. Repeat with the right hand point, forming a cone shape, with both ends meeting neatly in the middle. Staple together at the wide end.

lime and white chocolate fingers

makes 18

250 g (9 oz/2 cups) **plain (all-purpose) flour**

1 teaspoon **baking powder**

145 g (5 oz/2/3 cup) **caster (superfine) sugar**

75 g (21/2 oz) **unsalted butter**, melted

2 tablespoons **lime juice**

grated **zest** from 2 **limes**

1 teaspoon **natural vanilla extract**

1 **egg**, lightly beaten

1 **egg yolk**

150 g (51/2 oz) **white chocolate**, chopped

Preheat the oven to 170°C (325°F/Gas 3). Lightly grease and flour two baking trays.

Sift the flour and baking powder into a large bowl and stir in the sugar. Whisk together the butter, lime juice, zest, vanilla, egg and egg yolk until combined. Add the butter mixture to the flour mixture and stir until a firm dough forms.

Take tablespoonfuls of the dough and, on a lightly floured board, roll into thin logs 12 cm (41/2 inches) long. Place on the prepared trays and bake for 10 minutes, or until firm, swapping the position of the trays halfway through cooking. Cool on the trays for 5 minutes, then remove to a wire rack to cool completely.

Put the chocolate in a small heatproof bowl. Sit the bowl over a small saucepan of simmering water, stirring frequently until the chocolate has melted. Take care that the base of the bowl doesn't touch the water.

To decorate the biscuits, place them close together on the wire rack (put a piece of paper towel under the rack to catch the drips) and, using a fork dipped into the melted chocolate, drizzle the chocolate over the biscuits. Leave to set.

Lime and white chocolate fingers will keep, stored in an airtight container, for up to 2 days. Undecorated biscuits will keep for up to 7 days in an airtight container, or up to 8 weeks in the freezer.

chocolate fudge sandwiches

makes 20–24

250 g (9 oz/2 cups) **plain (all-purpose) flour**

30 g (1 oz/1/4 cup) **unsweetened cocoa powder**

200 g (7 oz) **unsalted butter**, chilled and diced

100 g (31/2 oz) **icing (confectioners') sugar**

2 **egg yolks**, lightly beaten

1 teaspoon **natural vanilla extract**

filling

100 g (31/2 oz/2/3 cup) chopped **dark chocolate**

1 tablespoon **golden syrup** or **dark corn syrup**

25 g (1 oz) **unsalted butter**, softened

Preheat the oven to 200°C (400°F/Gas 6). Lightly grease two baking trays.

Sift the flour and cocoa powder into a bowl and rub in the butter until the mixture resembles fine breadcrumbs. Sift in the icing sugar and stir to combine. Using a wooden spoon, gradually stir in the egg yolks and vanilla until a soft dough forms.

Transfer the dough to a lightly floured work surface and shape into a 4 x 6 x 26 cm (11/2 x 21/2 x 101/2 inch) block. Wrap in plastic wrap and chill for 30 minutes, or until firm. Cut the dough into 40–48 slices, about 5 mm (1/4 inch) wide. Place the slices, spacing them well apart, on the baking trays. Bake for 10 minutes, or until firm. Cool on the trays for 5 minutes, then transfer to a wire rack to cool completely.

To make the filling, put the chocolate in a small heatproof bowl. Sit the bowl over a small saucepan of simmering water, stirring frequently until the chocolate has melted. Take care that the base of the bowl doesn't touch the water. Remove from the heat, stir in the golden syrup and butter and continue stirring until the mixture is smooth. Allow to cool a little, then put in the refrigerator and chill for 10 minutes, or until the mixture is thick enough to spread. Use the chocolate filling to sandwich the biscuits together.

Filled biscuits are best eaten on the day they are made. Unfilled biscuits will keep, stored in an airtight container, for up to 3 days.

thumbprint biscuits

makes about 45

250 g (9 oz) **unsalted butter**, softened

140 g (5 oz) **icing (confectioners') sugar**

1 **egg yolk**, lightly beaten

90 g (3¼ oz) **cream cheese**, softened and cut into chunks

1½ teaspoons **natural vanilla extract**

1 teaspoon finely grated **lemon zest**

350 g (12 oz/2¾ cups) **plain (all-purpose) flour**, sifted

¼ teaspoon **baking powder**

½ teaspoon **bicarbonate of soda (baking soda)**

2 tablespoons each **apricot, blueberry and raspberry jam**

Preheat the oven to 180°C (350°F/Gas 4) and grease three baking trays.

Cream the butter, icing sugar and egg yolk in a bowl using electric beaters until pale and fluffy, then beat in the cream cheese, vanilla and lemon zest until smooth. Combine the flour, baking powder, bicarbonate of soda and ¼ teaspoon salt in a large bowl and, using a wooden spoon, gradually stir into the creamed mixture until a soft dough forms. Set aside for 5–10 minutes, or until the dough firms up.

Break off small (15 g/½ oz) pieces of dough, shape into balls and flatten slightly to make 4 cm (1½ inch) rounds. Transfer to the prepared trays and make a small indent in the centre of each with your thumb. Spoon about ¼ teaspoon of apricot jam into one-third of the biscuits, ¼ teaspoon blueberry jam into one-third, and ¼ teaspoon of raspberry jam into the remaining one-third of the biscuits. Bake for 10–12 minutes, or until light golden. Cool for a few minutes on the trays, then transfer to a wire rack.

These biscuits are best eaten the same day but will keep, stored in an airtight container, for up to 2 days.

walnut and orange biscotti

makes about 40

250 g (9 oz/2¹/2 cups) **walnut halves,** lightly toasted

310 g (11 oz/2¹/2 cups) **plain (all-purpose) flour,** plus extra for rolling

1 teaspoon **baking powder**

¹/2 teaspoon **bicarbonate of soda (baking soda)**

170 g (6 oz/³/4 cup) **caster (superfine) sugar**

3 **eggs,** lightly beaten

grated **zest** from 3 **oranges**

2 teaspoons **natural vanilla extract**

Preheat the oven to 170°C (325°F/Gas 3). Lightly grease a baking tray.

Roughly chop the walnuts and set aside. Sift the flour, baking powder and bicarbonate of soda into a large bowl, then stir in the sugar. Combine the eggs, orange zest and vanilla in a bowl and stir with a fork to mix well. Pour the egg mixture into the flour mixture and stir until nearly combined, then, using your hands, knead briefly to form a firm dough. Put the dough on a lightly floured work surface and knead the walnuts into the dough.

Divide the dough into three even-sized pieces. Working with one piece of dough at a time, roll each piece to form a 29 cm (11¹/2 inch) log. Gently pat the surface to flatten the log to a 4 cm (1¹/2 inch) width, then place on the prepared tray and bake for 30 minutes, or until light golden and firm. Remove from the oven and allow to cool for 15 minutes.

Reduce the oven to 150°C (300°F/Gas 2). When the logs are cool enough to handle, remove to a board and, using a sharp, serrated knife, cut the logs on the diagonal into 1 cm (¹/2 inch) thick slices. Arrange in a single layer on the two baking trays and bake for 15 minutes, swapping the position of the trays halfway through cooking, or until the biscotti are dry. Cool on a wire rack.

Biscotti will keep, stored in an airtight container, for up to 3 weeks.

cranberry and hazelnut refrigerator biscuits

makes about 50

125 g (4¹/2 oz/1 cup) **icing (confectioners') sugar**, sifted

175 g (6 oz) **unsalted butter**, softened

2 **egg yolks**

2 teaspoons **lemon juice**

185 g (6¹/2 oz/1¹/2 cups) **plain (all-purpose) flour**, sifted

110 g (3³/4 oz/1 cup) **ground hazelnuts**

150 g (5¹/2 oz/1¹/2 cups) **sweetened dried cranberries**

80 g (2³/4 oz/¹/2 cup) **poppy seeds**

Cream the icing sugar and butter in a bowl until pale and fluffy. Add the egg yolks and lemon juice and beat to combine well. Add the flour and ground hazelnuts and stir to combine well, then stir in the cranberries. Divide the mixture in half.

Scatter half the poppy seeds over a 30 cm (12 inch) long piece of foil. Place one half of the mixture on the work surface and form into a 21 cm (8 inch) long sausage shape. Transfer the dough to the foil, firmly rolling the dough in the poppy seeds to coat, then roll tightly in the foil to form a neat cylinder, twisting the ends tight. Repeat with the remaining poppy seeds and dough and another piece of foil. Refrigerate the dough for a minimum of 4 hours, but it can be left for up to 5 days.

When you are ready to bake the biscuits, preheat the oven to 170°C (325°F/Gas 3). Lightly grease two baking trays. Remove the foil and, using a large serrated knife, cut the dough into 8 mm (3/8 inch) thick slices. Place the rounds on the baking trays and bake for 12–15 minutes, or until firm and lightly coloured. Cool on the trays for 5 minutes, then transfer to a wire rack.

An uncooked log of dough can be frozen, ready to be thawed, sliced and baked, when needed. Cooked, the biscuits will keep, stored in an airtight container, for up to 1 week.

vanilla glazed rings

makes 40–44

125 g (41/2 oz) **unsalted butter**, softened

115 g (4 oz) **caster (superfine) sugar**

2 teaspoons **natural vanilla extract**

1 **small egg**, lightly beaten

200 g (7 oz/12/3 cups) **plain (all-purpose) flour**

1/2 teaspoon **baking powder**

1 quantity **icing glaze** (page 174)

yellow food colouring (optional)

1 quantity **royal icing** (page 174)

Preheat the oven to 180°C (350°F/Gas 4). Lightly grease two baking trays.

Cream the butter, sugar and vanilla in a bowl using electric beaters, then add the egg, beating well. Sift in the flour, baking powder and a pinch of salt and stir with a wooden spoon to form a dough.

Break off small pieces of dough and roll out each piece on a lightly floured work surface to form a 10 cm (4 inch) log. Curl into a ring and gently press the ends together. Transfer to the prepared baking trays and bake for 10–12 minutes, or until light golden. Cool briefly on the tray, then transfer to a wire rack to cool.

Make the icing glaze, adding a little yellow food colouring (if using) to the glaze. Make the royal icing and spoon into an icing bag (or see tip, page 177, to make your own paper icing bag).

Using a paintbrush, brush the tops of the biscuits with the glaze and leave to set on a wire rack. Pipe the royal icing backwards and forwards across the biscuits to form a zigzag pattern and leave to set.

The vanilla glazed rings will keep, stored in airtight container, for up to 3 days.

Break off **small pieces** of dough and roll out to form a 10 cm (4 inch) **log**.

Drizzle **the icing** over the tops of the **biscuits**.

marzipan pockets

makes 25

250 g (9 oz/2 cups) **plain (all-purpose) flour**, plus 2 1/2 teaspoons, extra

115 g (4 oz/1/2 cup) **caster (superfine) sugar**

200 g (7 oz) **unsalted butter**, chopped

3 **eggs**, separated

200 g (7 oz) good-quality **marzipan**, chopped

slivered almonds, for decoration

Combine the flour and sugar in a bowl, add the butter and, using your fingertips, rub in the butter until the mixture resembles breadcrumbs. Lightly beat the egg yolks in a small bowl, then stir into the flour mixture using a fork. Knead lightly with your hands just until a dough forms. Cut the dough in half, cover each piece with plastic wrap and refrigerate for 2 hours, or until firm.

Meanwhile, process the marzipan in a food processor until very finely chopped. Add the extra flour and 1 1/2 tablespoons of egg white and process until combined. Transfer the mixture to a small bowl, cover with plastic wrap and refrigerate.

Preheat the oven to 180°C (350°F/Gas 4). Lightly grease and flour two baking trays.

Remove the dough from the refrigerator and roll out on a lightly floured work surface to 4 mm (1/4 inch) thick. Using a 6.5 cm (2 1/2 inch) pastry cutter, cut out rounds from the dough, reserving the scraps. Put 25 of the rounds on the tray, brush lightly with some of the remaining egg white and place 1 teaspoon of marzipan mixture in the centre of each. Reroll the scraps and cut out more rounds, if needed, until you have a total of 25 more rounds. Place these on top of the rounds on the trays, pressing the edges lightly to seal.

Brush the tops with egg white. Using a small, sharp knife, make a small cut in the top of each. Scatter lightly with slivered almonds, then bake for 12–15 minutes, or until light golden. Cool on the trays for 5 minutes, then transfer to a wire rack to cool completely.

Marzipan pockets will keep, stored in an airtight container, for up to 5 days.

marsala and fennel seed rings

makes 24

375 g (13 oz/3 cups) **plain (all-purpose) flour**

55 g (2 oz/1/4 cup) **caster (superfine) sugar**

1 1/2 teaspoons **baking powder**

1 tablespoon **fennel seeds**

1 teaspoon **sea salt flakes**

80 ml (2 1/2 fl oz/1/3 cup) **sweet marsala**

125 ml (4 fl oz/1/2 cup) **extra virgin olive oil**

1 **egg yolk**

Preheat the oven to 180°C (350°F/Gas 4). Lightly grease a baking tray.

Combine the flour, sugar, baking powder, fennel seeds and sea salt in a bowl and stir to combine well.

Combine the marsala, olive oil and 80 ml (2 1/2 fl oz/1/3 cup) water in a bowl and whisk to combine. Add to the dry ingredients, then stir until a dough forms. Turn the dough out onto a work surface (the dough shouldn't stick, so there is no need to flour the surface) and divide in half. Cut each half into 12 even-sized pieces, then roll each into a 10 cm (4 inch) long log. Form each log into a ring, pressing the joins firmly to seal. Place on the prepared tray.

To make a glaze, mix the egg yolk with 1 tablespoon water. Brush the rings with the egg yolk glaze, then bake for 20 minutes. Reduce the oven to 150°C (300°F/Gas 2) and bake for another 15–20 minutes, or until golden and crisp. Cool on a wire rack. Serve with chunks of parmesan or pecorino cheese.

These rings will keep, stored in an airtight container, for up to 2 weeks.

sesame and ginger wafers

makes 18

40 g (1 1/2 oz) **unsalted butter**

40 g (1 1/2 oz) **caster (superfine) sugar**

2 tablespoons **golden syrup** or **dark corn syrup**

40 g (1 1/2 oz/1/3 cup) **plain (all-purpose) flour**

1/2 teaspoon **ground ginger**

1 tablespoon **brandy**

2 teaspoons **lemon juice**

1 tablespoon **sesame seeds**, toasted

Preheat the oven to 190°C (375°F/Gas 5). Grease two baking trays.

Combine the butter, sugar and syrup in a small saucepan and heat gently until the butter has melted and the mixture is smooth. Remove from the heat. Sift the flour and ginger into a bowl. Add the melted butter mixture and the brandy, lemon juice and sesame seeds and stir to mix well.

Drop 2 teaspoonfuls of the mixture (1 teaspoon for each wafer) onto each of the baking trays, leaving enough room between the mixture to allow for spreading. Using a palette knife, spread each one out to form a 10 cm (4 inch) round. Bake for 3–4 minutes, or until the wafers begin to brown around the edges, then remove from the oven.

Cool for 1 minute. Using the palette knife and working quickly, carefully remove the warm biscuits from the tray, then drape them over a rolling pin (you can use bottles and glasses as well) to make them curl. Cool completely, then remove from pin. Repeat with the remaining mixture.

Sesame and ginger wafers are best eaten on the day they are made.

bake it

oatcakes

makes 30–32

400 g (14 oz/3¹/4 cups) **fine oatmeal**

100 g (3¹/2 oz/²/3 cup) **oat bran**

1 teaspoon **bicarbonate of soda (baking soda)**

60 g (2¹/4 oz) **butter**, melted

Preheat the oven to 200°C (400°F/Gas 6). Lightly grease two baking trays.

Combine the oatmeal, oat bran, bicarbonate of soda and 1 teaspoon salt in a bowl. Make a well in the centre and, using a wooden spoon, stir in the melted butter and 250 ml (9 fl oz/1 cup) water to form a firm, slightly sticky dough.

Transfer the dough to a lightly floured work surface and knead until smooth. Roll out on a floured surface to a 2 mm (¹/16 inch) round and, using a 7 cm (2³/4 inch) pastry cutter, cut out rounds from the dough (rerolling the pastry scraps to press out a total of 30–32 rounds).

Transfer to the baking trays and bake for 18–20 minutes, or until the edges are lightly browned. Cool on trays for 5 minutes, then transfer to a wire rack to cool. Serve with cheeses, such as a blue cheese or aged cheddar.

Oatcakes will keep, stored in an airtight container, for up to 1 week.

coconut macaroons

makes about 64

4 **egg whites**, lightly beaten

450 g (1 lb/2 cups) **caster (superfine) sugar**

1 1/2 tablespoons **liquid glucose**

1 1/2 teaspoons **natural vanilla extract**

180 g (6 oz/2 cups) **desiccated coconut**

125 g (4 1/2 oz/1 cup) **plain (all-purpose) flour**

Combine the egg whites, sugar and liquid glucose in a large heatproof bowl and whisk to combine. Place the bowl over a saucepan of simmering water and whisk until the mixture is just warm. Remove from the heat and add the vanilla, coconut and flour and stir to combine well. Cover the bowl with plastic wrap and refrigerate the mixture until firm.

Meanwhile, preheat the oven to 150°C (300°F/Gas 2). Line two baking trays with baking paper.

Take a heaped teaspoonful of the mixture and, using wet hands, form the mixture into balls. Flatten the balls slightly and place them on the trays, spacing them apart. Bake for 15 minutes, or until the macaroons are light golden, swapping the position of the trays halfway through cooking. Cool for 5 minutes on the tray, then transfer to a wire rack to cool completely.

Macaroons will keep, stored in an airtight container, for up to 1 week, or frozen for up to 8 weeks.

tip Use large baking trays, if you have them, as you will need to give the macaroons room to spread. Alternatively, cook them in two batches.

bake it

rosewater meringues with raspberry cream

makes 30 'sandwiches'

4 **egg whites**

235 g (8¹/2 oz/1 cup) **caster (superfine) sugar**

1 tablespoon **rosewater**

a few drops of **pink food colouring** (optional)

icing (confectioners') sugar, for dusting

sugared rose petals (optional)

2–3 unsprayed **pink** or **red roses**

1 **egg white**, lightly beaten

115 g (4 oz/1/2 cup) **caster (superfine) sugar**

raspberry cream

300 ml (10¹/2 fl oz) **thick (double/heavy) cream**

1 tablespoon **icing (confectioners') sugar**, sifted

100 g (3¹/3 oz) **fresh raspberries,** or **frozen raspberries**, thawed

Following the circles drawn **on the** baking paper, pipe the meringue mixture into small **rounds**.

Use **a small** paintbrush to lightly brush the **egg white** on both sides of the petal.

Preheat the oven to 120°C (235°F/Gas 1/2). Line two baking trays with baking paper and mark thirty 3 cm (1 1/4 inch) rounds on each sheet of paper.

Whisk the egg whites in a clean, dry bowl until stiff peaks form. Add the sugar gradually, whisking well after each addition. Whisk until the mixture is stiff and glossy and the sugar has dissolved. Add the rosewater and food colouring, if using, to tint the meringue pale pink.

Transfer the mixture, in batches if necessary, to a piping bag fitted with a 1 cm (1/2 inch) plain nozzle. Following the marked rounds as a guide, pipe sixty 3 cm (1 1/4 inch) rounds, each about 2 cm (3/4 inch) high, onto the paper. Bake for 1 hour, then turn off the oven and leave the meringues to cool in the oven with the door slightly ajar.

To make sugared rose petals, if using, remove the petals from the roses. Working on one petal at a time, use a small paintbrush to lightly brush the egg white over both sides of the petal. Toss lightly in the sugar and set aside to dry. Repeat with the remaining petals. If not using immediately, store in an airtight container.

To make the raspberry cream, beat the cream and icing sugar until thick, then fold in the raspberries. Spread the raspberry cream over the bases of half the meringues and then join together with the remaining meringues to make a 'sandwich'. Decorate with the sugared rose petals, if using, and dust lightly with icing sugar. Serve immediately.

Unfilled meringues will keep, stored in an airtight container in a cool place, for up to 2 weeks.

orange polenta biscuits

makes 20–22

125 g (41/2 oz) **unsalted butter**, softened

80 g (23/4 oz/1/3 cup) **caster (superfine) sugar**

1 teaspoon **orange flower water**

finely grated **zest** from 1 **orange**

2 **eggs**, lightly beaten

165 g (53/4 oz/11/3 cups) **plain (all-purpose) flour**

80 g (23/4 oz/1/2 cup) **polenta (cornmeal)**

Preheat the oven to 200°C (400°F/Gas 6). Line two baking trays with baking paper.

Combine the butter, sugar, orange flower water and orange zest in a food processor and process until light and creamy. Add the eggs and process until smooth. Add the flour and polenta and pulse until a sticky dough forms.

Transfer the mixture to a piping bag fitted with a 2 cm (3/4 inch) star nozzle. Pipe the mixture onto the prepared baking trays to form 7 cm (23/4 inch) crescents. Bake for 15 minutes, or until the biscuits are golden around the edges. Cool on the trays for 5 minutes, then transfer to a wire rack to cool completely.

Orange polenta biscuits will keep, stored in an airtight container, for up to 3 days.

cumin seed wafers

makes 48

250 g (9 oz/2 cups) **plain (all-purpose) flour**

1 teaspoon **baking powder**

60 g (2¹/4 oz) **Copha (white vegetable shortening)**, chilled

1 tablespoon **cumin seeds**, toasted

Preheat the oven to 180°C (350°F/Gas 4). Lightly grease two baking trays.

Sift the flour, baking powder and 1 teaspoon salt into a bowl. Rub in the Copha until the mixture resembles fine breadcrumbs. Stir in the cumin seeds. Make a well in the centre of the mixture and gradually add 125 ml (4 fl oz/¹/2 cup) water, stirring with a wooden spoon until a dough forms. Knead the dough gently on a lightly floured work surface until just smooth. Cover with plastic wrap and refrigerate for 30 minutes.

Divide the dough into quarters and roll out each quarter on a floured work surface until 1 mm (¹/16 inch) thick, then trim the sides to form a 20 x 30 cm (8 x 12 inch) rectangle. Cut in half down the length, then cut across the width to form 5 cm (2 inch) wide fingers. You should end up with 12 fingers from each quarter of dough. Place on the baking trays and bake in batches for 10–12 minutes, or until light golden. Transfer to a wire rack to cool.

These wafers will keep, stored in an airtight container, for up to 1 week.

tip Take care when dry-roasting cumin seeds, as they can burn quite quickly. Place the seeds in a dry, heavy-based frying pan over low heat and heat just until fragrant.

bake it

chocolate, raisin and peanut clusters

makes about 40

200 g (7 oz) **dark chocolate**

60 g (21/4 oz) **unsalted butter**, chopped

170 g (6 oz/3/4 cup) **caster (superfine) sugar**

1 tablespoon **golden syrup** or **dark corn syrup**

11/2 teaspoons **natural vanilla extract**

155 g (51/2 oz/11/4 cups) **raisins**

200 g (7 oz/11/4 cups) **peanut halves**, toasted and roughly chopped

40 g (11/2 oz/1/3 cup) **plain (all-purpose) flour**

2 tablespoons **unsweetened cocoa powder**

Preheat the oven to 170°C (325°F/Gas 3). Lightly grease two baking trays.

Roughly chop 80 g (23/4 oz) of the chocolate and put in a heatproof bowl along with the butter, sugar, golden syrup and vanilla. Put the bowl over a saucepan of simmering water, stirring until the chocolate and butter have melted and the mixture is smooth. Take care that the base of the bowl doesn't touch the water. Allow to cool slightly.

Roughly chop the remaining chocolate and combine with the raisins and peanuts in a large bowl. Sift the flour and cocoa powder over the peanut mixture and toss to combine. Add the melted chocolate mixture and, using a wooden spoon, stir until the mixture is well combined and a firm dough forms.

Using a tablespoon of the mixture at a time, form into rough rounds, then place on the trays, spacing the biscuits about 4 cm (11/2 inches) apart. Bake for 15 minutes, swapping the position of the trays halfway through cooking, or until the biscuits are firm and no longer glossy. Cool on the trays for 5 minutes, then carefully remove to a wire rack to cool completely.

The chocolate biscuits will keep, stored in an airtight container, for up to 1 week, or frozen for up to 8 weeks.

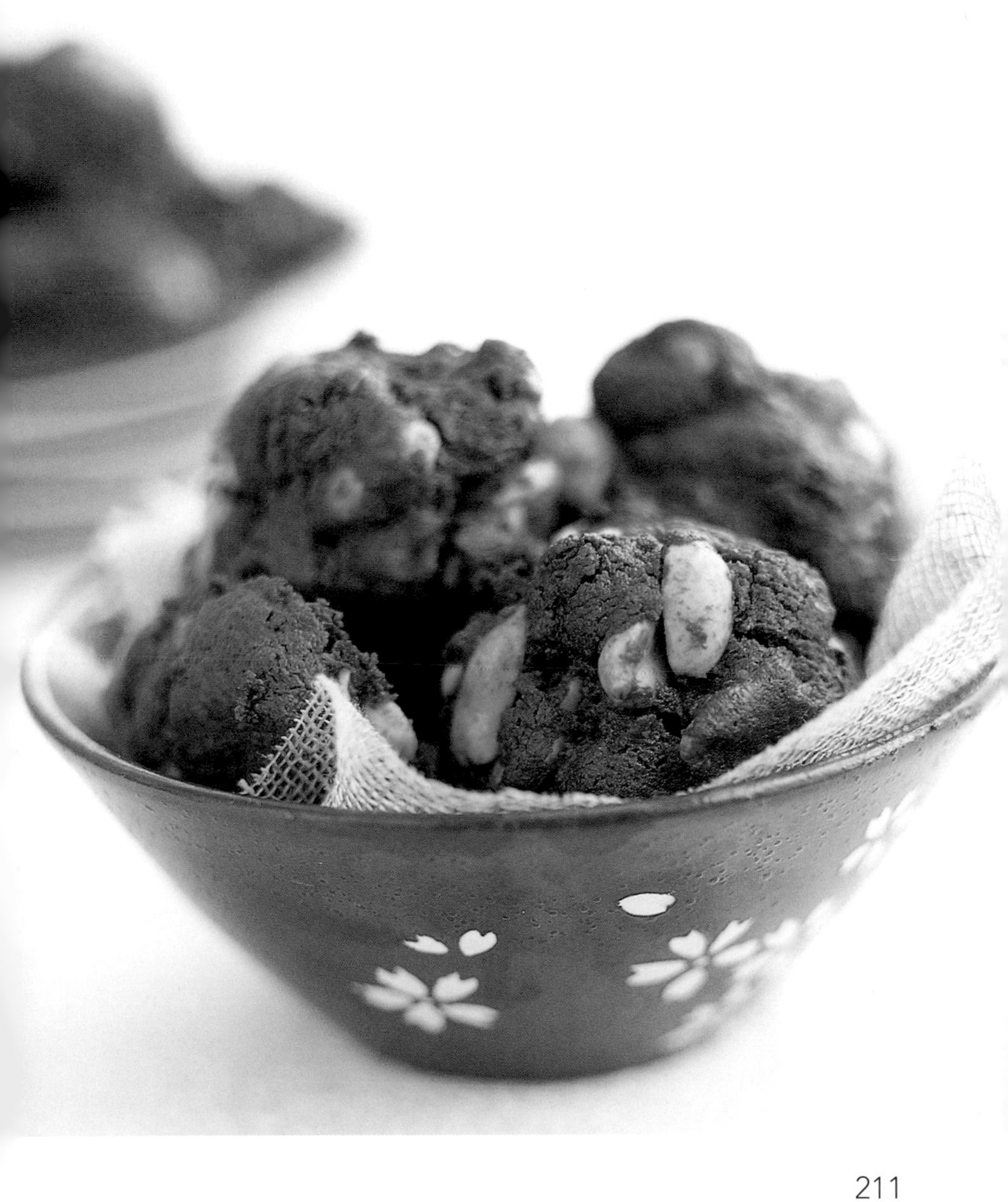

chocolate and cinnamon alphabet biscuits

makes about 32

125 g (4¹/2 oz) **unsalted butter,** softened

115 g (4 oz) **caster (superfine) sugar**

1 **egg**, lightly beaten

1/2 teaspoon **natural vanilla extract**

225 g (8 oz) **plain (all-purpose) flour**

30 g (1 oz/1/4 cup) **unsweetened cocoa powder**

1/2 teaspoon **baking powder**

2 teaspoons **ground cinnamon**

1 **egg white**

1 tablespoon **caster (superfine) sugar,** extra

1 teaspoon **ground cinnamon**

Preheat the oven to 190°C (375°F/Gas 5). Lightly grease two baking trays.

Cream the butter and sugar in a bowl using electric beaters until pale and fluffy, then beat in the egg and vanilla. Sift in the flour, cocoa powder, baking powder and cinnamon and, using a wooden spoon, stir into the creamed mixture until a soft dough forms. Cover the dough with plastic wrap and refrigerate for 30 minutes.

Roll out the dough between two sheets of baking paper to 5 mm (1/4 inch) thick, then cut out the letters using alphabet cutters.

To make a glaze for the biscuits, whisk the egg white with a fork until frothy, then set aside. Combine the extra sugar and ground cinnamon in a small bowl.

Brush the tops of the biscuits with the glaze, scatter over the cinnamon sugar and bake for 10 minutes, or until browned. Cool on the trays for 2 minutes, then transfer to a wire rack to cool completely.

The biscuits will keep, stored in airtight container, for up to 1 week.

bars and slices

about bars and slices

Part biscuit, part cake, bars and slices are a combination of ingredients baked in a tin and served cut into small pieces. Recipes for one of the most well-known and well-loved bars — the American classic, the chocolate brownie — first appeared around the late 1890s in North America and actually contained no chocolate at all: it was the use of molasses that gave them their colour and, most likely, their name. Bars and slices are popular in many cultures throughout the culinary world. Every Australian household instantly recognizes the chocolate-and-coconut-coated lamington. The Scottish sometimes make their shortbread in a rectangular tin to be served cut into fingers, as do the English with their moist, dense gingerbread cake. The wonderful flourless nut cakes popular in Middle Eastern and Eastern Mediterranean countries are baked in large trays and soaked with syrup while still hot. These delicious morsels are cut into diamonds to be enjoyed with a strong aromatic coffee.

bars and slices today

Bars and slices are also called tray bakes or fingers, and they are always baked in a shallow-sided cake tin, either square or rectangular. Somewhere between a biscuit, a pastry and a cake, a bar can be as simple as an all-in-one batter poured into a cake tin, baked, cooled and cut into pieces. Or they can be more decadent affairs, an assembly of layers baked together or separately, with or without a crust, sometimes iced or bathed in fragrant syrup. Shortcrust pastry provides a crisp base for a creamy caramel topping or softened fruits layered with a dome of feathery light meringue. Others surprise with a delicate layer of fruit sandwiched between a light airy sponge, crying out for a huge spoonful of crème fraîche. Bars can also be nutty, fruity health food snacks.

Whatever the ingredients, a bar is bar because of the way it is cooked and served. A baking tray, cake tin or flan tin is first lined with a layer of baking paper. Once cooked and then cooled, the mixture is lifted out of the tin and cut into the desired shapes — bars, fingers, diamonds or squares.

Cake-like in many ways, bars can be eaten as a delicious mid-morning snack or with afternoon tea. Topped with a spoonful of whipped cream or drizzled with vanilla bean custard, bars make wickedly good desserts. Flavours are varied and textures diverse; bars can be soft and chewy, moist or dense and even crisp. As diverse as they are delicious, bars provide an intensely rich and luscious sweet treat.

hints and tips

- Buy good quality, sturdy, non-stick baking tins. Always use the size of tin recommended in the recipe to ensure the cooking times are accurate.

- Line trays or tins with baking paper so that the paper extends over the two long sides. This makes it easier to lift the cooled mixture out of the tin to cut into slices.

- If you use a food processor to make the pastry, use it only to rub the fat into the flour. After adding the liquid, pulse briefly until the mixture just comes together, then turn out onto a work surface and gently shape the dough into a ball. It is really important not to overwork pastry dough or it will be tough when cooked.

- A soft pastry dough can be rolled out between two sheets of baking paper to prevent it from sticking to the work surface.

- If the dough is too soft to be rolled out, it may be necessary to press it into the tin. Once pressed well into the base and edges of the tin, use the back of a spoon to smooth the surface as flat and evenly as possible.

- When bars and slices are made with several layers, it is important that each layer is completely cold before adding the next one.

- If short on time, the bar can be made in two stages. After lining the tin with pastry, chill overnight, wrapped loosely in plastic wrap, ready to finish the next day.

- Bars should only be iced when cooled completely.

- Allow the cooked mixture to cool before slicing it, unless specified.

- If the cooked mixture is quite sticky and difficult to cut, run the blade of the knife under hot or boiling water before cutting.

apricot meringue squares

makes 24 pieces

250 g (9 oz/2 cups) **plain (all-purpose) flour**
1 1/2 teaspoons **ground cinnamon**
60 g (2 1/4 oz/1/2 cup) **icing (confectioners') sugar**
200 g (7 oz) **unsalted butter**, chopped

apricot filling

200 g (7 oz) chopped **dried apricots**
80 g (2 3/4 oz/1/3 cup) **caster (superfine) sugar**

meringue topping

2 **egg whites**
80 g (2 3/4 oz/1/3 cup) **caster (superfine) sugar**
115 g (4 oz/1 1/4 cups) **desiccated coconut**

Press the **dough** evenly into the tin, using the back of a **spoon**.

Spoon the cooled **apricot mixture** evenly over the cooked base.

Preheat the oven to 180°C (350°F/Gas 4). Lightly grease a 20 x 30 cm (8 x 12 inch) rectangular shallow tin and line the base with baking paper, leaving the paper hanging over on the two long sides.

Combine the flour, cinnamon and icing sugar in a food processor and process until just combined. Add the butter and, using the pulse button, pulse until the mixture is crumbly. Add 1–1 1/2 tablespoons water and process until the mixture just forms a dough; do not overprocess. Using the back of a spoon, press the dough evenly into the prepared tin. Refrigerate for 20 minutes.

Bake the dough for 15–20 minutes, or until golden. Remove from the oven and allow to cool.

Meanwhile, to make the apricot filling, combine the apricots, sugar and 250 ml (9 fl oz/1 cup) water in a small saucepan. Stir over medium heat until the sugar has dissolved, then reduce the heat and simmer for 12 minutes, or until the mixture is thick. Remove from the heat and cool, then spread over the cooled base.

To make the topping, whisk the egg whites in a clean, dry bowl until soft peaks form. Gradually add the sugar, whisking well after each addition. Whisk until the mixture is stiff and glossy and the sugar has dissolved. Fold in the coconut. Spread the topping evenly over the filling. Bake for 15 minutes, or until the topping is just firm to touch. Cool completely before cutting into 5 x 5 cm (2 x 2 inch) squares.

The apricot meringue squares will keep, stored in an airtight container, for up to 4 days.

date and cinnamon squares

makes 36

600 g (1 lb 5 oz/3¹/3 cups) **pitted whole dried dates,** chopped

1 teaspoon **bicarbonate of soda (baking soda)**

125 g (4¹/2 oz) **unsalted butter,** chopped

155 g (5¹/2 oz/2/3 cup) **soft brown sugar**

2 **eggs**

125 g (4¹/2 oz/1 cup) **plain (all-purpose) flour**

60 g (2¹/4 oz/¹/2 cup) **self-raising flour**

¹/2 teaspoon **ground cinnamon,** plus ¹/2 teaspoon, extra

60 g (2¹/4 oz/¹/2 cup) **icing (confectioners') sugar**

Preheat the oven to 180°C (350°F/Gas 4). Lightly grease a 23 cm (9 inch) square shallow tin and line the base with baking paper.

Combine the dates and 500 ml (17 fl oz/2 cups) water in a medium saucepan, bring to the boil, then remove from the heat. Stir in the bicarbonate of soda and mix well. Cool to room temperature.

Cream the butter and sugar in a large bowl using electric beaters until pale and fluffy. Add the eggs one at a time, beating well after each addition. Sift the flours and cinnamon into a bowl, then fold into the butter mixture alternately with the date mixture. Spread into the prepared tin. Bake for 55–60 minutes, or until a skewer inserted into the centre comes out clean. Cool in the tin for 5 minutes, then turn out onto a wire rack to cool completely.

Cut into 36 pieces and place on a sheet of greaseproof paper. Sift the combined icing sugar and extra cinnamon over the cubes and toss to coat. Serve immediately (the coating will be absorbed into the cakes quite quickly if left to stand).

Date and cinnamon squares will keep (do not coat with the icing sugar if you intend to store them), stored in an airtight container, for up to 4 days, or up to 3 months in the freezer.

honey and almond slice

makes about 30

base

215 g (7¹/2 oz/1³/4 cups) **plain (all-purpose) flour**

150 g (5¹/2 oz) **unsalted butter**, chopped

90 g (3¹/4 oz/³/4 cup) **icing (confectioners') sugar**

1 **egg**, lightly beaten

filling

125 g (4¹/2 oz) **unsalted butter**

125 g (4¹/2 oz) **caster (superfine) sugar**

2 **eggs**

30 g (1 oz/¹/4 cup) **plain (all-purpose) flour**

155 g (5¹/2 oz/1¹/2 cups) **ground almonds**

topping

90 g (3¹/4 oz) **unsalted butter**, chopped

80 g (2³/4 oz/¹/3 cup) **caster (superfine) sugar**

1¹/2 tablespoons **honey**

125 g (4¹/2 oz/1 cup) **slivered almonds**

Preheat the oven to 180°C (350°F/Gas 4). Lightly grease a 20 x 30 cm (8 x 12 inch) rectangular tin and line the base with baking paper, leaving the paper hanging over on the two long sides.

To make the base, combine the flour, butter and icing sugar in a food processor and process until the mixture resembles fine breadcrumbs. Add the egg and process until a dough forms; do not overprocess. Using lightly floured hands, press the dough evenly over the base of the tin. Bake for 10 minutes, or until light golden. Cool slightly before adding the filling.

Meanwhile, to make the filling, cream the butter and sugar in a bowl using electric beaters until pale and fluffy. Add the eggs one at a time, beating well after each addition. Fold in the flour and ground almonds, then spread the mixture over the partly cooked base. Bake for 16–18 minutes, or until golden and firm to the touch. Set aside to cool.

To make the topping, put the butter, sugar, honey and almonds in a saucepan and stir over low heat until the butter melts and the sugar dissolves. Increase the heat, then boil the mixture for 3 minutes, or until it starts to come away from the side of the saucepan. Working quickly and using an oiled metal spatula or palette knife, spread the mixture over the filling. Bake for a further 10 minutes, or until golden brown. Cool in the tin, then lift out and cut into squares.

Honey and almond slice will keep, stored in an airtight container, for up to 5 days.

Using floured hands, **press** the dough into the base of **the tin**.

Working quickly, spread the **almond** mixture over the top of the **filling**.

cashew brownies

makes 25

200 g (7 oz) **dark chocolate**, chopped

175 g (6 oz) **unsalted butter**, chopped

2 **eggs**

230 g (8¹/2 oz/1 cup) **soft brown sugar**

40 g (1¹/2 oz/¹/3 cup) **unsweetened cocoa powder**

125 g (4¹/2 oz/1 cup) **plain (all-purpose) flour**

80 g (2³/4 oz/¹/2 cup) **unsalted cashews**, toasted and chopped

100 g (3¹/2 oz) **dark chocolate**, chopped, extra

icing

200 g (7 oz) **dark chocolate**, chopped

125 g (4¹/2 oz/¹/2 cup) **sour cream**

30 g (1 oz/¹/4 cup) **icing (confectioners') sugar**, sifted

Preheat the oven to 160°C (315°F/Gas 2–3). Lightly grease a 23 cm (9 inch) square shallow tin and line the base with baking paper.

Put the chocolate and butter in a heatproof bowl. Sit the bowl over a saucepan of simmering water, stirring frequently until the chocolate and butter have melted. Take care that the base of the bowl doesn't touch the water. Allow to cool.

Whisk the eggs and sugar in a large bowl for 5 minutes, or until pale and thick. Fold in the cooled chocolate mixture, then the sifted cocoa powder and flour. Fold in the cashews and extra chocolate, then pour into the tin, smoothing the top. Bake for 30–35 minutes, or until just firm to the touch. (The brownies may have a slightly soft centre when hot but will firm when cool.) Allow to cool.

To make the icing, put the chocolate in a small heatproof bowl. Sit the bowl over a small saucepan of simmering water, stirring frequently until the chocolate has melted. Take care that the base of the bowl doesn't touch the water. Allow to cool slightly, then add the sour cream and icing sugar and stir to mix well. Spread evenly over the cooled brownies. Leave for a few hours or overnight to firm up, then cut into squares.

The brownies will keep, stored in an airtight container, for up to 5 days, or up to 3 months in the freezer.

semolina syrup slice

makes 25

55 g (2 oz/1/2 cup) **ground almonds**

170 g (6 oz/2/3 cup) **plain yoghurt**

230 g (8 oz/1 cup) **caster (superfine) sugar**

125 g (41/2 oz) **unsalted butter**, melted

1/2 teaspoon **natural vanilla extract**

2 **eggs**, lightly beaten

185 g (61/2 oz/11/2 cups) **semolina**

1 teaspoon **baking powder**

2 tablespoons whole **unsalted pistachio nuts**, for decoration

syrup

170 g (6 oz/3/4 cup) **caster (superfine) sugar**

1 teaspoon finely grated **lemon zest**

1 tablespoon **lemon juice**

Preheat the oven to 180°C (350°F/Gas 4). Lightly grease a 23 cm (9 inch) square shallow tin and line the base with baking paper.

To make the syrup, combine the sugar, lemon zest and lemon juice in a saucepan with 125 ml (4 fl oz/1/2 cup) water. Stir over low heat until the sugar has dissolved. Increase the heat, bring the mixture to the boil and simmer for 10 minutes without stirring. Allow to cool, then strain.

Put the ground almonds in a small frying pan and stir over medium heat for 3–5 minutes, or until lightly browned, then remove from the heat and cool.

Combine the yoghurt and sugar in a bowl, stir until well combined, then stir in the butter, vanilla and eggs. Combine the semolina and baking powder in a bowl, stir to mix well, then stir into the yoghurt mixture along with the almond mixture. Spread the mixture over the base of the prepared tin, smoothing the surface, then arrange the pistachios evenly over the top. Bake for about 35 minutes, or until the top is lightly browned and a skewer inserted into the centre comes out clean. Pour the cold syrup over the hot slice. Leave to cool completely in the tin before cutting into squares.

The slice will keep, stored in an airtight container, for up to 3 days.

glacé fruit fingers

makes 20

60 g (2¹/4 oz/¹/2 cup) **plain (all-purpose) flour**

2 tablespoons **self-raising flour**

2 tablespoons **icing (confectioners') sugar**

60 g (2¹/4 oz) **unsalted butter**, chopped

1 **egg yolk**

topping

350 g (12 oz) assorted light-coloured **glacé fruits**
   (pineapple, apricots, peaches, pears)

80 ml (2¹/2 fl oz/¹/3 cup) **brandy**

175 g (6 oz) **unsalted butter**, softened

115 g (4 oz/¹/2 cup) **caster (superfine) sugar**

2 tablespoons **honey**

1 **egg**

40 g (1¹/2 oz/¹/3 cup) **plain (all-purpose) flour**

40 g (1¹/2 oz/¹/3 cup) **self-raising flour**

80 g (2³/4 oz/¹/2 cup) **macadamia nuts**, toasted and chopped

icing (confectioners') sugar, for dusting (optional)

Preheat the oven to 180°C (350°F/Gas 4). Lightly grease a 20 x 30 cm (8 x 12 inch) rectangular shallow tin and line the base with baking paper, leaving the paper hanging over on the two long sides.

Process the flours and icing sugar in a food processor until just combined. Add the butter and, using the pulse button, process in short bursts until the mixture is crumbly. Add the egg yolk and about 1 tablespoon water and pulse just until a dough forms. Cover with plastic wrap and refrigerate for 30 minutes.

Roll out the pastry between two sheets of baking paper until large enough to cover the base of the tin. Transfer to the tin.

To make the topping, cut the fruit into 5 mm (1/4 inch) pieces with scissors or a sharp knife. Combine the fruit and brandy in a bowl, mix well and leave, covered, for about 1 hour, or until the fruit has absorbed the brandy.

Cream the butter, sugar and honey in a small bowl using electric beaters until pale and fluffy. Add the egg and beat well until combined. Sift the flours together in a bowl, then stir into the creamed mixture. Stir in the glacé fruit and macadamia nuts, then spread the mixture evenly over the pastry. Bake for 30–35 minutes, or until golden brown. The topping may be slightly soft but will firm on cooling. Cool in the tin, then cut into 7.5 x 4 cm (3 x 11/2 inch) pieces and dust lightly with icing sugar before serving.

Glacé fruit fingers will keep, stored in an airtight container, for up to 4 days, or frozen for up to 3 months.

tip If preferred, you could use dried fruit, such as dried pears, peaches and mango, instead of glacé fruit.

Cut the glacé fruits into
small pieces using
kitchen scissors.

Stir in **the fruit** and
macadamia nuts.

cardamom pear shortcake

makes 20

250 g (9 oz) **dried pears**

1 tablespoon **caster (superfine) sugar**

275 g (9³/4 oz) **unsalted butter**, chopped

140 g (5 oz/³/4 cup) lightly packed **soft brown sugar**

80 g (2³/4 oz/¹/3 cup) **caster (superfine) sugar**

3 **eggs**

280 g (10 oz/2¹/4 cups) **plain (all-purpose) flour**

1 teaspoon **baking powder**

1 teaspoon **ground cardamom**

icing (confectioners') sugar, for dusting

Preheat the oven to 180°C (350°F/Gas 4). Lightly grease a 20 x 30 cm (8 x 12 inch) rectangular shallow tin with butter and line with baking paper, leaving the paper hanging over on the two long sides.

Put the dried pears in a bowl, cover with boiling water and soak for several hours, or until the pears have softened a little and the water has cooled. Drain off the water, reserving 125 ml (4 fl oz/¹/2 cup). Put the pears and sugar in a saucepan with the reserved soaking water. Stir to dissolve the sugar, then return to the boil and cook, covered, for 5 minutes, or until the pears are soft.

Cream the butter and sugars in a bowl using electric beaters until pale and fluffy. Add the eggs one at a time, beating well after each addition. Sift over the flour, baking powder and cardamom, then, using a large metal spoon, fold the flour mixture into the butter mixture until well combined. Spread half the mixture evenly over the base of the prepared tin. Scatter the pears over, then dot the remaining mixture over the pears to cover.

Bake for 40–45 minutes, or until golden and a skewer inserted into the centre of the cake comes out clean. Leave to cool in the tin, then carefully lift out, dust with icing sugar and cut into 10 x 3 cm (4 x 1¹/4 inch) fingers.

The cardamom pear shortcake will keep, stored in an airtight container in a cool place, for up to 3 days.

orange and almond slice

makes 12

30 g (1 oz) **rice flour**

40 g (1¹/2 oz/¹/3 cup) **cornflour (cornstarch)**

60 g (2¹/4 oz/¹/2 cup) **ground almonds**

2 tablespoons **icing (confectioners') sugar**

60 g (2¹/4 oz) **unsalted butter**, chopped

filling

1 **small orange**

1 **egg**, separated

55 g (2 oz/¹/4 cup) **caster (superfine) sugar**

80 g (2³/4 oz/³/4 cup) **ground almonds**

1 tablespoon **caster (superfine) sugar**, extra

lemon icing

90 g (3¹/4 oz/³/4 cup) **icing (confectioners') sugar**

1 teaspoon **unsalted butter**

1–1¹/2 tablespoons **lemon juice**

Grease the base and sides of **a rectangular** fluted tart **tin**.

Sit the bowl over a saucepan of simmering water and stir until **the icing** is smooth.

Preheat the oven to 180°C (350°F/Gas 4). Lightly grease the base and sides of a 35 x 11 cm (14 x 4¼ inch) loose-based rectangular shallow tart tin.

Combine the rice flour, cornflour, almonds and icing sugar in a food processor and process briefly to just combine. Add the butter and, using the pulse button, process in short bursts just until a dough forms. Press the dough into the base of the tin, then refrigerate for 30 minutes.

Meanwhile, to make the filling, put the orange in a small saucepan with enough water to cover. Bring to the boil, then reduce the heat, cover and simmer for 30 minutes, or until soft. Drain and cool. Cut the orange in half widthways, remove any seeds, and process in a food processor until smooth.

Whisk the egg yolk and sugar in a bowl for 5 minutes, or until pale and thick, then fold in the orange purée and almonds. Using clean beaters, whisk the egg white in a clean, dry bowl until stiff peaks form. Add the extra sugar, beating until well combined, then fold into the orange mixture. Gently spread the filling over the base. Bake for 40 minutes, or until lightly browned. Cool in the tin, then remove.

To make the lemon icing, combine the sifted icing sugar and butter in a heatproof bowl with enough juice to form a thick paste. Sit the bowl over a saucepan of simmering water, stirring until the icing is smooth and runny, then remove from the heat. Working quickly, spread the icing evenly over the filling, then leave to set. Cut into 2.5 cm (1 inch) thick slices.

The slice will keep, stored in an airtight container, for up to 4 days.

lemon squares

makes 24

base

185 g (6¹/2 oz/1¹/2 cups) **plain (all-purpose) flour**, sifted

60 g (2¹/4 oz/¹/2 cup) **icing (confectioners') sugar**

180 g (6 oz) **unsalted butter**, chopped

topping

6 **eggs**, lightly beaten

460 g (1 lb/2 cups) **caster (superfine) sugar**

2 teaspoons finely grated **lemon zest**

250 ml (9 fl oz/1 cup) **lemon juice**

60 g (2¹/4 oz/¹/2 cup) **plain (all-purpose) flour**

icing (confectioners') sugar, for dusting

Preheat the oven to 170°C (325°F/Gas 3). Lightly grease a 20 x 30 cm (8 x 12 inch) rectangular shallow tin with butter and line the base with baking paper, leaving the paper hanging over on the two long sides.

To make the base, mix the flour and icing sugar in a bowl. Using your fingertips, rub in the butter until the mixture resembles breadcrumbs. Press the dough evenly over the base of the tin. Bake for 25 minutes, or until golden and firm to the touch. Set aside to cool. Reduce the oven to 160°C (315°F/Gas 2–3).

To make the topping, whisk the eggs and sugar in a bowl for 3–4 minutes, or until pale and thick. Whisk in the lemon zest and juice, then add the flour and whisk to just combine. Pour the mixture over the base and bake for 45 minutes, or until set, covering with foil for the last 20 minutes of cooking. Cool in the tin, then carefully lift out and cut into 5 cm (2 inch) squares using a hot knife. Dust with icing sugar just before serving.

The lemon squares will keep, stored in an airtight container in the refrigerator, for up to 3 days.

cheese and sultana slice

makes about 25

base

125 g (4¹/2 oz) **unsalted butter**, chopped

70 g (2¹/2 oz/¹/2 cup) **icing (confectioners') sugar**, plus extra for dusting

185 g (6¹/2 oz/1¹/2 cups) **plain (all-purpose) flour**, sifted

topping

250 ml (9 fl oz/1 cup) **milk**

30 g (1 oz) **unsalted butter**

150 g (5¹/2 oz) **soft goat's cheese**, crumbled

100 g (3¹/2 oz) **cream cheese**, chopped

1 teaspoon finely grated **lemon zest**

60 ml (2 fl oz/¹/4 cup) **lemon juice**

2 tablespoons **caster (superfine) sugar**

30 g (1 oz/¹/4 cup) **cornflour (cornstarch)**

60 g (2¹/4 oz/¹/2 cup) **sultanas (golden raisins)**, chopped

3 **egg whites**

80 g (2³/4 oz/¹/3 cup) **caster (superfine) sugar**, extra

Preheat the oven to 180°C (350°F/Gas 4). Lightly grease a 20 x 30 cm (8 x 12 inch) rectangular shallow tin with butter and line the base with baking paper, leaving the paper hanging over on the two long sides.

To make the base, cream the butter and icing sugar in a bowl until pale and fluffy. Add the flour and stir until a dough forms. Using lightly floured hands, press the dough evenly over the base of the tin. Bake for 15–20 minutes, or until golden and firm to the touch. Cool.

To make the topping, combine the milk, butter, cheeses, lemon zest, lemon juice and sugar in a large saucepan and stir over medium heat for 5 minutes, or until the butter and cheeses have melted and the mixture is smooth. Combine the cornflour and 60 ml (2 fl oz/1/4 cup) cold water in a small bowl and stir until smooth. Add to the cheese mixture, then, whisking continuously, bring to the boil and cook, stirring, for 3–4 minutes, or until thickened. Remove from the heat and stir in the sultanas. Set aside.

Whisk the egg whites in a clean, dry bowl until stiff peaks form. Add the sugar gradually, whisking well after each addition. Whisk until the mixture is stiff and glossy and the sugar has dissolved. Carefully fold the egg whites into the cheese mixture and mix until just combined. Spread the mixture over the cooled base. Bake for 25–30 minutes, or until firm to the touch and golden brown. Cool completely in the tin, then carefully lift out and, using a hot knife, cut into diamonds. Dust with icing sugar to serve.

The cheese slice is best served on the day it is made.

tip For best results, use freshly squeezed lemon juice and not the ready-squeezed lemon juice available in bottles.

Stir over low heat until the **butter** and **cheeses** have melted.

When the **mixture** has thickened, remove from **the** heat and whisk in the sultanas.

honey caramel slice

makes 20

base

200 g (7 oz) **unsalted butter**, chopped

310 g (11 oz/2¹/2 cups) **plain (all-purpose) flour**

115 g (4 oz/¹/2 cup) **caster (superfine) sugar**

2 **egg yolks**, lightly beaten

filling

2 x 395 g (14 oz) cans **sweetened condensed milk**

100 g (3¹/2 oz) **unsalted butter**, chopped

115 g (4 oz/¹/3 cup) **honey**

Preheat the oven to 180°C (350°F/Gas 4). Lightly grease a 20 x 30 cm (8 x 12 inch) rectangular shallow tin with butter and line the base with baking paper, leaving the paper hanging over on the two long sides.

To make the base, combine all the ingredients, except the egg yolks, in a food processor and process until the mixture resembles fine breadcrumbs. Add the yolks and 1–2 tablespoons chilled water and process just until a dough forms, adding a little more water if necessary; do not overprocess. Using lightly floured hands, press half the dough over the base of the tin. Bake for 12–15 minutes, or until golden and firm to the touch. Wrap the remaining dough in plastic wrap and refrigerate until firm.

To make the filling, put the condensed milk and butter in a heavy-based saucepan and stir over low heat until the butter has melted. Increase the heat to medium and cook for 5–8 minutes, stirring continuously, or until the mixture has thickened. Remove from the heat and stir in the honey. Allow to cool, then pour the filling over the base and spread evenly to cover.

Using a grater, grate the cold dough over the caramel filling to cover, then bake for 20–30 minutes, or until golden. Cool in the tray, then carefully lift out and cut into 10 x 3 cm (4 x 1¹/4 inch) fingers.

The honey caramel slice will keep, stored in an airtight container, for up to 3 days.

mocha lamingtons

makes 25

125 g (41/2 oz) **unsalted butter**, chopped, softened

230 g (8 oz/1 cup) **caster (superfine) sugar**

1/2 teaspoon **natural vanilla extract**

2 **eggs**

250 g (9 oz/2 cups) **self-raising flour**

250 ml (9 fl oz/1 cup) **milk**

2 teaspoons **instant coffee**, dissolved in 2 teaspoons boiling water

icing

375 g (13 oz/3 cups) **icing (confectioners') sugar**

60 g (21/4 oz/1/2 cup) **unsweetened cocoa powder**

20 g (3/4 oz) **unsalted butter**

2 teaspoons **instant coffee powder**

75 g (21/2 oz/11/4 cups) **shredded coconut**

90 g (31/4 oz/1 cup) **desiccated coconut**

Dip the squares of cake into the **chocolate** icing.

Roll the **iced cake** in the coconut to thoroughly **cover it**.

Preheat the oven to 180°C (350°F/Gas 4). Lightly grease the base of a 23 cm (9 inch) square shallow tin and line the base with baking paper.

Cream the butter, sugar and vanilla in a bowl using electric beaters until pale and fluffy. Add the eggs one at a time, beating well after each addition. Sift the flour into a bowl, then stir the flour into the butter mixture alternately with the milk until combined and smooth. Spoon half the mixture into the prepared tin and spread evenly over the base. Add the dissolved coffee to the remaining mixture and stir until well combined. Carefully spread the coffee mixture over the mixture in the tin.

Bake for 30–35 minutes, or until a skewer inserted into the centre of the cake comes out clean. Cool in the tin for 5 minutes before turning out onto a wire rack to cool. Cut into 25 squares.

To make the icing, sift the icing sugar and cocoa powder into a large shallow bowl. Add the butter and coffee and gradually whisk in 150 ml (5 fl oz) boiling water until smooth. Put the shredded and desiccated coconuts in a large shallow bowl and toss to combine.

Using two spoons to hold the cake, dip the cake squares into the icing to cover, allowing the excess to drip off. (Add a little boiling water to the icing if it starts to thicken). Roll the cake in the coconut to cover and place on a wire rack. Repeat with the remaining cakes.

tip The cake for the lamingtons is best made 1 day in advance — it will be easier to cut and won't crumble as much. The cake is best coated in the chocolate and coconut on the day of serving.

rhubarb slice

makes about 25

300 g (10½ oz) **rhubarb**, trimmed and cut into 5 mm (¼ inch) slices

115 g (4 oz/½ cup) **caster (superfine) sugar**

185 g (6½ oz) **unsalted butter**, chopped

230 g (8 oz/1 cup) **caster (superfine) sugar**

½ teaspoon **natural vanilla extract**

3 **eggs**

90 g (3¼ oz/¾ cup) **plain (all-purpose) flour**

¾ teaspoon **baking powder**

1 tablespoon **sugar**

icing (confectioners') sugar, for dusting

Combine the rhubarb and sugar in a bowl and set aside, stirring occasionally, for 1 hour, or until the rhubarb has released its juices and the sugar has dissolved. Strain well, discarding the liquid.

Preheat the oven to 180°C (350°F/Gas 4). Lightly grease a 20 x 30 cm (8 x 12 inch) rectangular shallow tin with butter. Line the base with baking paper, leaving the paper hanging over on the two long sides.

Cream the butter, sugar and vanilla in a bowl using electric beaters until pale and fluffy. Add the eggs one at a time, beating well after each addition. Sift the flour and baking powder over the mixture, then stir to combine. Spread the mixture evenly over the base of the prepared tin, then put the rhubarb over the top in a single layer. Sprinkle with the sugar. Bake for 40–45 minutes, or until golden. Leave to cool slightly in the tin, then carefully lift out and cut into squares. Dust with icing sugar and serve warm as a dessert with cream, or at room temperature as a snack.

The rhubarb slice is best eaten on the day it is made.

pastry

about pastry

Pastry-making is closely related to bread- and cake-making, although it is perhaps a later addition than most other forms of baking. The Romans made thin sheets of dough, similar to filo pastry, not to eat, but to cover meats to keep them moist as they cooked. It was the Northern Europeans in medieval times who first began to produce edible pastries, made with solid fats such as butter and lard. But it wasn't until the 15th century that pastry-making became part of Western culinary tradition. In the 1420s a French cook was the first to incorporate butter into a flour and water dough, producing a flaky pastry similar to what we use today. From the 16th century, specific recipes for pastries began to appear, and from the middle of the 18th century, pastries were promoted as an art in their own right. French and Swiss pastry chefs, in particular, were skilled in the art and many speciality pastry shops were opened, showcasing their magnificent goods in spectacular displays.

pastry today

Today, pastries come in all shapes, sizes and flavours. We use a wide range of different pastry doughs to contain a combination of delicious sweet and savoury fillings. Pastries may come in many guises but they all share the same wonderful characteristics — they are at once tender and flaky, light and creamy, mouthwatering and delicate.

The success to good pastry lies in the perfect combination of a meltingly crisp crust and the sublime filling it encases. We use pastry to make tart cases, which are frequently baked blind (pre-baked) to ensure crispness, and pies, with their golden domed lids, hiding a mass of delicious soft fruits. Then there are those little feathery light pastries rolled or layered with nuts or fragrant spices, providing the perfect snack or appetizer.

Making pastry at home can appear daunting to a beginner, but it really is simple providing you follow a few rules and get to know your ingredients. Recipes in this book use five different types of pastry:

shortcrust: The simplest and most versatile dough. It is made with flour and butter and just enough water to bind. The texture, once cooked, is light and crisp and it can be used in both sweet and savoury pastries.

sweet shortcrust: This is shortcrust pastry enriched with eggs and sugar, and used only in sweet dishes. Eggs help bind as well as add richness, and sugar sweetens the dough and provides extra crispness. Sweet shortcrust has a crumbly, biscuit-like texture.

choux pastry: Made in a pan over heat and beaten firmly to incorporate air. Because it is a soft batter it is never rolled out, but is piped or spooned onto a baking tray. During cooking the mixture rises and the crust sets, leaving a hollow centre. This is then filled with a sweet or savoury filling.

puff pastry and filo pastry: Because making these pastries can be quite challenging for the home cook, all recipes in this book recommend the use of commercial products (see page 263). These are readily available frozen from most supermarkets.

essential ingredients

flour

The best type of flour to use for making shortcrust, sweet shortcrust and choux pastry is plain (all-purpose) flour, made from a combination of hard and soft wheat varieties. Wheat flour is the only flour that contains sufficient gluten to allow pastry to stretch and expand in the oven. Different brands and, even, batches of flour absorb water at different rates, so always add water to flour gradually to avoid the dough becoming too wet. Add a little more water if the mixture is too dry.

fat

Butter gives pastry a wonderful rich flavour and also makes it tender. Unsalted butter is preferable, as the pastry can then be used to make either sweet or savoury dishes. It is important when making shortcrust and sweet shortcrust that the butter is chilled before it is rubbed into the flour.

liquid

Water binds the flour and butter together and also provides moisture. It should be well chilled before adding to shortcrust dough.

eggs

Both whole eggs and egg yolks are used in pastry doughs. The yolks add richness and a crumbly texture, as well as colour; whole eggs bind the flour, making it more pliable. In choux pastry, eggs also aerate the dough as they are beaten in, helping it to rise.

sugar

Sugar is added both to sweeten dough and to give a crisp result. Because sugar caramelizes as it cooks, pastry can scorch if left too long in the oven, so watch carefully as it bakes. Although caster (superfine) sugar is most frequently used in pastry-making, icing (confectioners') sugar is also used, especially in sweet shortcrust.

ready-made puff pastry

Puff pastry consists of literally hundreds of layers of dough interlaced with butter. It is sold frozen in block form, or in ready-rolled sheets. Defrost the block pastry and roll out according to the recipe. The pastry sheets can usually be separated while still frozen, so you can thaw just the quantity required for a particular recipe. Always choose butter puff pastry, as the flavour and texture are superior to that made with commercial margarines.

ready-made filo pastry

Filo pastry is available fresh or frozen and is sold in packets of rolled sheets. If using frozen filo, you will need to thaw the whole packet to remove the required amount of sheets. Because filo pastry is exceptionally delicate, the sheets will crack and tear if allowed to dry out. Take one sheet at a time and keep the remainder covered with a clean, damp tea towel (dish towel) until required. Always butter or oil the pastry immediately to prevent it from drying out.

shortcrust pastry

makes 380 g (13 1/2 oz)

200 g (7 oz/1 2/3 cups) **plain (all-purpose) flour**, sifted

120 g (4 1/4 oz) chilled **unsalted butter**, chopped

If making pastry using a food processor, put the flour, butter and 1/4 teaspoon salt in the food processor. Using the pulse button, process until the mixture resembles course breadcrumbs.

Add 60 ml (2 fl oz/1/4 cup) chilled water, adding the water gradually, and pulse just until a dough forms, being careful not to overprocess. If the dough is dry and not coming together, add a little more water, 1 teaspoon at a time. As soon as the mixture comes together, turn out onto a lightly floured work surface and press into a flat, round disc. Cover with plastic wrap and refrigerate for 30 minutes.

If making the pastry by hand, sift the flour and salt into a large bowl and add the butter. Using your fingertips, rub the butter into the flour until the mixture resembles coarse breadcrumbs. Make a well in the centre.

Pour 60 ml (2 fl oz/1/4 cup) chilled water into the well, then stir with a flat-bladed knife to incorporate the water. When the mixture starts to come together in small beads of dough, gently gather the dough together and lift it out onto a lightly floured work surface. Gently press the dough together into a ball, kneading it lightly if necessary until the dough comes together. Press into a flat, round disc, cover with plastic wrap and refrigerate for 30 minutes. The dough is now ready to use. Roll out the dough and proceed as directed in the recipe.

sweet shortcrust pastry

makes 400 g (14 oz)

200 g (7 oz/1²/3 cups) **plain (all-purpose) flour**, sifted

85 g (3 oz/²/3 cup) **icing (confectioners') sugar**, sifted

100 g (3¹/2 oz) chilled **unsalted butter**, chopped

1 **egg yolk**

If making pastry using a food processor, put the flour, icing sugar, butter and a pinch of salt in the food processor. Using the pulse button, process until the mixture resembles coarse breadcrumbs.

Combine the egg yolk with 1 tablespoon chilled water in a small bowl. Add to the flour mixture and, using the pulse button, process until a dough forms, being careful not to overprocess. If the dough is dry and not coming together, add a little more water, 1 teaspoon at a time. Turn out onto a lightly floured work surface and press the dough into a flat, round disc. Cover with plastic wrap and refrigerate for 30 minutes.

If making the pastry by hand, sift the flour, icing sugar and a pinch of salt into a large bowl, then add the butter. Using your fingertips, rub the butter into the flour until the mixture resembles course breadcrumbs. Make a well in the centre.

Combine the egg yolk with 1 tablespoon chilled water in a small bowl. Pour it into the well, then stir with a flat-bladed knife. When the mixture starts to come together in small beads of dough, gently gather the dough together and lift it out onto a lightly floured work surface. Gently press the dough together into a ball, then press into a flat, round disc. Cover with plastic wrap and refrigerate for 30 minutes. The dough is now ready to use. Roll out the dough and proceed as directed in the recipe.

bake it

making shortcrust

If making **shortcrust** pastry using a food processor, use the **pulse** button to process the ingredients just until a dough forms.

Use your **hands** to press the dough into a flat disc, then **chill in the** refrigerator for 30 minutes.

If making shortcrust pastry by **hand**, rub the butter into the dry **ingredients** until the mixture resembles **breadcrumbs**.

Pour the chilled **water** into the bowl and stir until the **mixture** starts to come together in small beads of dough.

lining a tart tin

Roll out the pastry, then carefully fold the **pastry** back over and around the **rolling pin** and lift it gently from the **surface**.

Unroll the **pastry** over the tin and ease it into the **tin**, pressing to fit the side. Roll the pin across the top to cut off the excess **dough**.

baking blind

Line the tart tin with baking paper, **then** pour in baking beads, uncooked **rice** or dried pulses, such as chickpeas **or lentils**.

Cook in a 200°C (400°F/Gas 6) oven **for** 15 minutes. Lift out the paper and beads and bake for 5 minutes. Remove from **the** oven ready for use.

choux pastry

makes about 40 choux puffs and 16 éclairs

100 g (3¹/2 oz) **unsalted butter**

1 teaspoon **caster (superfine) sugar**

140 g (5 oz) **plain (all-purpose) flour**

3 **eggs**

Preheat the oven to 200°C (400°F/Gas 6). Lightly grease or line a baking tray with baking paper.

Put 250 ml (9 fl oz/1 cup) water, the butter and sugar in a small saucepan and heat until the butter has melted and the mixture has just come to the boil. Add the flour and, using a wooden spoon, stir over medium heat until the mixture comes away from the side of the saucepan, forming a ball.

Place the mixture into the bowl of an electric mixer fitted with a whisk attachment and allow to cool slightly. Add the eggs one at a time, beating well after each addition and waiting until each egg is incorporated before adding the next. (Alternatively, you can use a hand mixer or wooden spoon to mix the ingredients.) The mixture should be thick and glossy. The pastry is now ready to use and may be piped, spooned or shaped according to the recipe you are using.

To make choux puffs, place teaspoonfuls of the mixture on baking trays spacing them 4 cm (1¹/2 inches) apart. Bake for 20 minutes, then reduce the heat to 160°C (315°F/Gas 2–3) and bake for a further 20 minutes, or until puffed, golden and dry (pull one puff apart to see if it is dry inside). Turn off the oven, open the door slightly, and leave the pastries in the oven until cool.

To make éclairs, put the choux pastry into a piping bag fitted with a 2 cm (3/4 inch) plain nozzle. Pipe 10 cm (4 inch) lengths of choux onto the baking tray, spacing them 4 cm (1¹/2 inches) apart. Bake as for choux puffs.

Pastries will keep, if stored in an airtight container, for up to 3 days. To refresh them, if necessary, place on a baking tray and heat in a preheated 180°C (350°F/Gas 4) oven for 5–10 minutes, or until the pastry is dry and crisp.

making choux pastry

Add the flour and stir until the **mixture** comes together to form **a ball**.

Add **the eggs** one at a time, whisking well after **each addition**.

If making **choux puffs**, spoon the mixture onto the tray, **leaving room** for spreading.

If making **éclairs**, pipe the **choux** into 10 cm (4 inch) lengths, spacing them a **little apart**.

hints and tips

shortcrust and sweet shortcrust

■ The kitchen needs to be as cool as possible when making pastry.

■ Pastry can be made in a food processor, so you needn't worry about hot or heavy hands, but it is really important not to overwork the dough or it will become tough.

■ Butter should be cold, straight from the refrigerator. Cut the butter into even-sized pieces, about 5 mm (1/4 inch) thick.

■ Always use chilled water to bind the dough.

■ Flour should be sifted before use. This will remove any lumps and incorporate air into the flour, helping to make the dough light. For sweet shortcrust, always sift icing sugar and flour to remove any lumps and help aerate them.

■ For sweet shortcrust, stir the egg yolks with chilled water before adding them to the flour and sugar.

■ If using a food processor, take care not to overprocess the dough or it will become tough.

■ Dough needs to covered completely with plastic wrap or it will dry out.

■ Always rest dough in the refrigerator for at least 30 minutes.

■ If the dough is too cold to roll out it will crack easily, so leave at room temperature, still covered in plastic wrap, for 15 minutes to soften.

■ Roll the pastry out on a lightly floured work surface to prevent it sticking. Always roll from the middle outwards (not using a back-and-forth motion) and rotate the pastry frequently as you go to keep to the required shape. Occasionally use both hands to gently push the edges of the dough back inwards to help keep the shape.

- If possible, use a marble slab or a cold work surface to roll dough. This helps prevent the butter from warming up as it is rolled.

- If the dough feels really soft and starts to stick to the work surface, roll it out between two sheets of baking paper.

- Never pull or stretch pastry as you roll it or the pastry will shrink during cooking.

- When baking blind, the pastry shell is first lined with a piece of crumpled baking paper. Crumbling the paper slightly helps it to better fit the shape of the pastry.

- Shortcrust (and sweet shortcrust) pastry keeps well once made. Cover with plastic wrap and refrigerate for up to 3 days. It also freezes for up to 3 months. The pastry can be rolled out and then frozen, either as a flat sheet on a baking tray lined with baking paper, or after it has been used to line the tin. Alternatively, freeze as a ball of dough.

choux pastry

- Always preheat the oven before beginning to make the choux pastry because it is cooked immediately after it is shaped or piped. Likewise, prepare your equipment before you start. Lightly grease or line the baking tray with baking paper. If piping the dough, fit a large plain nozzle to the piping bag.

- Add the flour to the boiling mixture in one go.

- Immediately beat the mixture with a wooden spoon to prevent lumps forming. Stop beating as soon as the soft dough comes away from the side of the pan and remove from the heat.

- Always allow the hot mixture to cool for 2–3 minutes before adding eggs or they can start to cook.

- Beat in the eggs one at a time, making sure they are completely beaten in before adding the next egg.

- The dough is ready when it is smooth and glossy. It should be piped or shaped while it is still warm. Leave about 4 cm (1½ inches) between the piped or spooned dough.

red wine and currant tart

serves 8

200 g (7 oz/1⅓ cups) **currants**

200 ml (7 fl oz) **red wine**

200 ml (7 fl oz) **blackcurrant juice**

½ teaspoon **lemon juice**

1 **cinnamon stick**

2 **cloves**

1 quantity **sweet shortcrust pastry** (page 267)

6 **eggs**

100 g (3½ oz) **caster (superfine) sugar**

20 g (¾ oz) **butter**, melted

icing (confectioners') sugar, for dusting

Preheat the oven to 200°C (400°F/Gas 6). Lightly grease a 28 cm (11¼ inch) loose-based round tart tin.

Put the currants in a heatproof bowl and set aside. Put the red wine, blackcurrant juice, lemon juice, cinnamon and cloves in a saucepan over medium heat and bring to a simmer. Remove the red wine mixture from the heat and strain the mixture onto the currants in the bowl. Leave the currants to soak in the liquid for 2 hours.

Roll out the pastry on a lightly floured work surface until 3 mm (⅛ inch) thick, to fit the base and side of the tart tin. Roll the pastry around the pin, lift and ease into the tin, gently pressing the side to fit, then trim the edges. Wrap the whole tin in plastic wrap and chill in the refrigerator for 1 hour.

Line the pastry shell with a crumpled piece of baking paper and cover the base with baking beads or uncooked rice. Bake the pastry for 10 minutes, then remove the paper and beads and bake for a further 8–10 minutes, or until the pastry is golden. Reduce the oven to 160°C (315°F/Gas 2–3).

Whisk the eggs with the sugar and butter in a bowl to combine well. Put the currant mixture in a saucepan and warm through, but do not allow it to boil. Pour the warm currant mixture over the egg mixture, stirring to combine. Pour into the tart base. Bake for 30–40 minutes, or until the filling is just set. Allow to cool a little, then serve lightly dusted with icing sugar.

coconut baklava

makes 24

360 g (12¾ oz/4 cups) **desiccated coconut**

1 teaspoon **ground cinnamon**

½ teaspoon **ground nutmeg**

a pinch of **ground cloves**

10 sheets **filo pastry** (about 150 g/ 5½ oz)

200 g (7 oz) **unsalted butter**, melted

syrup

400 g (14 oz/1¾ cups) **caster (superfine) sugar**

1½ tablespoons **lemon juice**

1½ tablespoons **honey**

1 tablespoon **orange blossom water**

Preheat the oven to 180°C (350°F/Gas 4). Lightly grease a 28 x 20 cm (11¼ x 8 inch) rectangular shallow tin and line the base with baking paper.

Put the coconut, cinnamon, nutmeg and cloves in a large bowl and stir to combine.

Cut the stack of filo sheets in half widthways, so it will fit into the tin. Brush a sheet of filo liberally with melted butter, top with another sheet and repeat until you have four layers of pastry. Repeat with the remaining filo to give five stacks in total, each with four layers.

Put one stack of filo in the tin and brush the top of the filo with butter. Evenly spread one-quarter of the coconut mixture over the filo, top with another filo stack and brush with butter. Repeat with remaining coconut mixture and pastry stacks, finishing with a layer of filo. Liberally brush the top with butter, then score into diamond shapes using a sharp knife, making the cuts about 1 cm (½ inch) deep (do not cut all the way through at this stage). Bake for 18–20 minutes, or until golden and crisp.

Meanwhile, make the syrup. Combine 400 ml (14 fl oz) water, the sugar, lemon juice, honey and orange blossom water in a saucepan and stir until the sugar dissolves. Bring to a simmer and cook for 10 minutes, or until slightly thickened. Cool the syrup.

While the baklava is still very hot, pour over the cold syrup. Allow to cool completely before cutting along the scored marks into diamond shapes to serve.

pear tart tatin

serves 8

145 g (5 oz/2/3 cup) **caster (superfine) sugar**

50 g (13/4 oz) **butter**, chopped

1/2 teaspoon **ground ginger**

1/2 teaspoon **ground cinnamon**

3 **beurre bosc pears**, peeled, cored and cut into wedges

450 g (1 lb) block **frozen butter puff pastry**, thawed

thick (double/heavy) cream, to serve

Preheat the oven to 220°C (425°F/Gas 7). Put a 22 cm (8½ inch) heavy-based frying pan with an ovenproof handle over medium heat. Add the sugar and heat, shaking the pan constantly, until the sugar is a dark caramel colour. Add the butter, ginger and cinnamon and stir to combine. Arrange the pears on top, spoon over the caramel to coat, then reduce the heat to low and cook, covered, for 5 minutes, or until the pears just begin to soften.

Remove the frying pan from the heat and arrange the pears over the base of the pan, overlapping them neatly to make a decorative finish when turned out. Leave to cool slightly.

Roll out the pastry on a lightly floured work surface to a 24 cm (9½ inch) round. Place the pastry over the pears in the frying pan, tucking the edges around the pears so they are enclosed in pastry. Bake for 20–25 minutes, or until the pastry is golden and puffed. Leave for 10 minutes, then run a knife around the edge of the pan to loosen the tart and invert it onto a serving platter. Serve warm with cream.

The tart is best served on the day it is made.

tip A cast-iron frying pan with an ovenproof handle works best for this tart, but you can use any heavy-based frying pan, as long as it is ovenproof.

Spoon the caramel sauce over the **pears** to coat.

Place the **pastry** round over the pears, tucking it down firmly at the **edges**.

palm sugar, lime and star anise coils

makes 24

2 **star anise**

60 g (2¼ oz) **palm sugar**, finely grated, or **soft brown sugar**

2 teaspoons **lime zest**

2 sheets ready-rolled **frozen butter puff pastry**, thawed

40 g (1½ oz) **butter**, melted

Preheat the oven to 200°C (400°F/Gas 6). Line a baking tray with baking paper.

Put the star anise in a small ovenproof dish and dry-roast in the oven for 5 minutes. Cool, then grind using a mortar and pestle to form a fine powder. Mix together the ground anise, palm sugar and lime zest in a small bowl.

Lay the two sheets of pastry on the work surface and brush each with some of the melted butter. Scatter the palm sugar mixture over the two sheets. Take one pastry sheet and roll it up firmly to form a long log. Repeat with the second pastry sheet. Cut each log into 12 even-sized slices, then put the slices on the baking tray, spacing them a little apart. Flatten each pastry slightly with the palm of your hand, then brush the tops with the remaining butter. Refrigerate for 30 minutes, then bake for 20 minutes, or until puffed and golden brown.

tip You could also use a clean coffee grinder to grind the roasted star anise.

freeform apple and cherry crostade

serves 8

20 g (3/4 oz) **butter**

3 **green apples**, peeled, cored and cut into 1 cm (1/2 inch) pieces

60 g (21/4 oz/1/3 cup) **soft brown sugar**

1/2 teaspoon **ground cinnamon**

1/2 teaspoon **ground ginger**

1/2 teaspoon **lemon juice**

2 tablespoons **plain (all-purpose) flour**

300 g (101/2 oz/2 cups) **pitted fresh, frozen or drained tinned cherries**

1 quantity **sweet shortcrust pastry** (page 267)

1 **egg yolk**

1 tablespoon **milk**

80 g (23/4 oz/1/4 cup) **apricot jam**

Preheat the oven to 180°C (350°F/Gas 4). Grease and flour a large baking tray.

Melt the butter in a saucepan over medium heat. Add the apples, brown sugar, cinnamon, ginger and lemon juice and cook, covered, for 5 minutes, or until the apples have softened a little. Remove from the heat, cool a little, then stir in the flour and cherries.

Roll out the pastry on a lightly floured work surface into a round 3 mm (1/8 inch) thick and place onto the prepared baking tray. Pile the apple and cherry filling into the centre of pastry, leaving a 5 cm (2 inch) border. Fold the pastry over the filling, leaving the centre uncovered, pleating the pastry to fit. Combine the egg yolk and milk to make a glaze and brush over the edges of the pastry. Bake the crostade on the bottom shelf of the oven for 35–40 minutes, or until golden.

To make a jam glaze, combine the apricot jam and 11/2 tablespoons water in a small saucepan and bring to a simmer, stirring to combine. Brush the glaze over the pastry and fruit. Let the crostade cool slightly before serving.

pink grapefruit meringue tartlets

makes 8

2 quantities **sweet shortcrust pastry** (page 267)

grapefruit curd
100 g (3½ oz) **butter**, chopped
6 **eggs**, lightly beaten
250 ml (9 fl oz/1 cup) **ruby grapefruit juice**
1 tablespoon finely grated **ruby grapefruit zest**
170 g (6 oz/¾ cup) **caster (superfine) sugar**

meringue
4 **egg whites**, at room temperature
115 g (4 oz/½ cup) **caster (superfine) sugar**
1 tablespoon **cornflour (cornstarch)**

Preheat the oven to 180°C (350°F/Gas 4). Lightly grease eight loose-based tartlet tins, 10 cm (4 inches) in diameter and 3 cm (1 1/4 inches) deep.

Roll out the pastry on a lightly floured work surface to 3 mm (1/8 inch) thick. Cut the pastry into rounds to fit the base and sides of the tins. Gently press the sides to fit, trim the edges, then wrap the tins in plastic wrap and refrigerate for 30 minutes.

Line each of the pastry shells with a crumpled piece of baking paper and fill with baking beads or uncooked rice. Blind bake the pastry for 10 minutes, then remove the paper and beads and bake for a further 5 minutes, or until the pastry is golden. Allow to cool.

To make the grapefruit curd, combine the butter, eggs, grapefruit juice, zest and sugar in a heatproof bowl. Place over a saucepan of simmering water and whisk constantly for 10–15 minutes, or until the mixture thickens. Set aside to cool. Spoon the curd into the tart shells, smoothing the top. Place in the refrigerator for 30 minutes, or until completely cold.

To make the meringue, whisk the egg whites in a clean, dry bowl until soft peaks form. Add the sugar, 1 tablespoon at a time, whisking well after each addition. Whisk until the mixture is stiff and glossy and the sugar has dissolved. Add the cornflour, whisking to mix well.

Place the mixture in a piping bag fitted with a 2 cm (3/4 inch) plain nozzle. Remove the tartlets from the refrigerator and pipe the meringue over the curd. Bake for 10 minutes, or until the meringue is golden.

tip Pastry is baked blind for several reasons. Firstly it ensures that the finished pastry is crisp, whatever type of filling it contains. A tart case is often cooked first so that it can be filled with a ready-cooked filling that only requires a short amount of baking (which wouldn't be sufficient to cook the pastry through).

Whisk the **egg whites** until soft peaks form. You can use **either** electric beaters or a balloon whisk to do this.

Use a piping bag to pipe the **meringue** over the top of the grapefruit **curd**.

espresso chocolate tart

serves 12

1 quantity **sweet shortcrust pastry** (page 267), made with 2 tablespoons finely
ground **coffee beans** substituted for 2 tablespoons of the flour

50 g (1¾ oz) **dark chocolate**, chopped

400 g (14 oz) **milk chocolate**, chopped

300 ml (10½ fl oz) **thick (double/heavy) cream**

Preheat the oven to 200°C (400°F/Gas 6). Grease a 35 x 11 cm (14 x 4¼ inch) loose-based rectangular shallow tart tin.

Roll out the pastry on a lightly floured work surface until 3 mm (⅛ inch) thick, to fit the base and sides of the tin. Roll the pastry around the pin, then lift and ease it into the tin, gently pressing to fit into the corners. Trim the edges, cover with plastic wrap and refrigerate for 1 hour.

Line the pastry shell with a crumpled piece of baking paper and cover the base with baking beads or uncooked rice. Bake the pastry for 10 minutes, then remove the paper and beads and bake for a further 10 minutes, or until the pastry is golden.

Put the dark chocolate in a small heatproof bowl. Sit the bowl over a small saucepan of simmering water, stirring frequently until the chocolate has melted and the mixture is smooth. Take care that the base of the bowl doesn't touch the water. Brush the base of the pastry with melted chocolate.

Put the milk chocolate and cream in a small heatproof bowl. Sit the bowl over a small saucepan of simmering water, stirring until the chocolate has melted and the mixture is smooth. Allow the chocolate to cool slightly, then pour into the tart case. Refrigerate overnight, or until the chocolate filling has set. Serve the tart in small slices as it is very rich.

cumin and gouda gougères

makes 40

100 g (3¹/2 oz) **butter**

140 g (5 oz) **plain (all-purpose) flour**

¹/2 teaspoon **cumin seeds**, lightly crushed

3 **eggs**

150 g (5¹/2 oz) **aged gouda cheese**, finely grated

Preheat the oven to 200°C (400°F/Gas 6). Line a baking tray with baking paper.

Heat 250 ml (9 fl oz/1 cup) water, the butter and ¹/4 teaspoon salt in a small saucepan over medium heat until the butter has melted and the mixture has just come to the boil. Add the flour and cumin and stir until the mixture comes away from the side of the saucepan. Transfer to the bowl of an electric mixer and allow to cool a little (alternatively use a hand mixer or wooden spoon). Beating continuously, add the eggs one at a time, beating well after each addition. Stir in the cheese.

Put teaspoonfuls of the mixture onto the prepared baking tray, spacing them about 4 cm (1¹/2 inches) apart. Bake for 20 minutes, then reduce the heat to 160°C (315°F/ Gas 2–3) and cook for a further 20 minutes, or until the gougères are puffed, golden and dry. Turn off the oven, open the door slightly and leave the gougères to cool a little. Serve warm or at room temperature, with drinks.

tip Gougères originated in Burgundy, traditionally as an accompaniment to the local wines. They can also be split and filled with savoury fillings, such as chicken or fish.

croquembouche with coffee cream filling

serves 10

1 quantity **choux pastry** (page 272), made into 40 choux puffs, cooled

700 g (1 lb 9 oz/3 cups) **caster (superfine) sugar**

coffee cream filling

1 1/2 tablespoons **instant coffee granules**

400 g (14 oz) **mascarpone**

60 g (2 1/4 oz/1/2 cup) **icing (confectioners') sugar**

2 tablespoons **pouring cream**

To make the coffee cream filling, dissolve the coffee in 1 tablespoon boiling water. Put the mascarpone, icing sugar, cream and coffee mixture in a bowl. Using electric beaters, combine well.

Place the filling in a piping bag fitted with a nozzle less than 1 cm (1/2 inch) in diameter. Using the end of a teaspoon, make a small hole in the base of each choux puff, then pipe the filling into the puffs.

To make a caramel, put the sugar and 250 ml (9 fl oz/1 cup) water in a heavy-based saucepan and slowly bring to a simmer over medium heat. Cook, without stirring, for 20 minutes, or until the mixture turns a deep caramel colour. Remove from the heat and immediately put the saucepan into a large bowl of cold water to stop the caramel cooking further.

To assemble, dip the base of three puffs into the caramel and place them together on a serving plate to form a triangular shape. Dip the base of a fourth puff into the caramel and place on top of the triangle, in the centre, to form a small pyramid. Repeat to make 10 individual pyramids in total.

Dip two forks into the remaining caramel, then rub the backs of the forks together until the caramel begins to stick. Gently pull the forks apart to check whether the caramel is cool enough to spin. If it drips, it probably needs longer to cool. When the caramel forms fine threads of toffee, spin it around each croquembouche until they are covered with fine threads of toffee. Serve immediately.

tip Croquembouche, meaning 'crunch in the mouth', is a traditional French dessert often served at celebrations such as weddings. If you prefer, you can assemble the puffs to make one large croquembouche. Start with a large circle of puffs at the base (an odd number of puffs seems to work best) and gradually assemble the layers to form a pyramid shape.

Make **a small** hole in the choux puffs and pipe the **coffee cream** filling into the **puffs**.

Rub **the forks** together until the caramel is tacky, then **gently pull** apart.

apple and amaretti pie

serves 8–10

2 quantities **sweet shortcrust pastry**
(page 267)
40 g (1 1/2 oz) **butter**
5 **green apples**, peeled, cored and
thinly sliced
1 teaspoon **lemon juice**
1/2 teaspoon **ground cinnamon**

80 g (2 3/4 oz/1/3 cup) **soft brown sugar**
25 g (1 oz/1/4 cup) **flaked almonds**,
toasted
50 g (1 3/4 oz/1 cup) roughly chopped
amaretti
1 **egg yolk**
icing (confectioners') sugar, for dusting

Preheat the oven to 200°C (400°F/Gas 6). Grease a 23 x 3 cm (9 x 1 1/4 inch) pie dish.

Using two-thirds of the pastry, roll it out on a lightly floured work surface until 3 mm (1/8 inch) thick, to fit the base and side of the dish. Roll the pastry around the pin, then lift and ease it into the dish. Trim the edges, cover with plastic wrap and refrigerate for 30 minutes. Roll out the remaining pastry until 3 mm (1/8 inch) thick, to fit the top of the dish. Put the pastry round onto a large plate, cover with plastic wrap and refrigerate for 30 minutes.

Line the pastry shell with a crumpled piece of baking paper and cover the base with baking beads or uncooked rice. Bake the pastry for 10 minutes, then remove the paper and beads and bake for a further 10 minutes, or until the pastry is golden. Remove from the oven and reduce the temperature to 180°C (350°F/Gas 4).

Melt the butter in a large saucepan, then add the apples, lemon juice, cinnamon and brown sugar and cook, covered, over medium heat for 5 minutes, or until the apple begins to soften. Remove from the heat and stir in the almonds and amaretti.

Spoon the mixture into the pastry shell. Combine the egg yolk with 1 tablespoon water and brush over the edge of the pastry. Cover with the pastry round, gently pressing the pastry together to seal the edges. Cut a small hole in the centre to allow steam to escape and brush the top with the egg wash. Bake for 45 minutes, or until the pastry is golden. Cool, then lightly dust with icing sugar to serve.

tip Amaretti are a light crisp Italian macaroon biscuit made with sweet and bitter almonds.

ginger and mango éclairs

makes 16

1 quantity **choux pastry** (page 272)

1 x 5 g (1/8 oz) **gelatine sheet**, or

   11/2 teaspoons **gelatine powder**

200 ml (7 fl oz) **puréed mango flesh**

1 teaspoon **lemon juice**

125 ml (4 fl oz/1/2 cup) **thick**

   (double/heavy) cream

30 g (1 oz/1/4 cup) **icing**

   (confectioners') sugar

ginger icing

60 g (21/4 oz/1/2 cup) **icing**

   (confectioners') sugar

10 g (1/4 oz) **unsalted butter**

1/2 teaspoon **ground ginger**

1/2 teaspoon **lemon juice**

Preheat the oven to 200°C (400°F/Gas 6). Line two baking trays with baking paper.

Put the choux pastry into a piping bag fitted with a 2 cm (3/4 inch) plain nozzle. Pipe 10 cm (4 inch) lengths of choux onto the baking tray, spacing them 4 cm (11/2 inches) apart. Bake for 20 minutes, then reduce the heat to 160°C (315°F/Gas 2–3) and bake for another 20 minutes, or until puffed, golden and dry. Turn off the oven, open the door slightly and leave the choux in the oven until cool.

If using the gelatine sheet, soak it in cold water for 5 minutes, or until softened, then squeeze out the excess moisture. If using gelatine powder, sprinkle the gelatine over 3 tablespoons water in a bowl. Leave the gelatine to sponge — it will swell. Combine the mango purée and lemon juice in a small heatproof bowl over simmering water. Add the softened gelatine sheet or sponged gelatine powder to the warm liquid, whisking to dissolve the gelatine. Remove from the heat, then refrigerate until the mixture is cool and beginning to thicken. Whisk the cream and icing sugar in a bowl until thick, then fold in the cooled mango mixture.

To make the ginger icing, combine the icing sugar, butter, ginger and lemon juice in a small bowl. Pour over 2 teaspoons boiling water and whisk until a smooth, thin icing forms, adding a few more drops of water if necessary. Without cutting all the way through, split the éclairs horizontally. Spoon about 1 tablespoon of filling into each, then drizzle the tops with ginger icing. Refrigerate until the icing sets.

Eclairs are best served on the day they are made.

potato, feta and roast garlic pasties

serves 8–10

300 g (10½ oz) **all-purpose potatoes** (such as pontiacs), unpeeled

8 **garlic cloves**

2 teaspoons **rosemary leaves,** chopped

2 tablespoons **extra virgin olive oil**

80 g (2¾ oz) **feta cheese,** crumbled

½ teaspoon grated **lemon zest**

sea salt

2 quantities **shortcrust pastry** (page 264)

1 **egg yolk**

1 tablespoon **milk**

Preheat the oven to 180°C (350°F/Gas 4). Lightly grease a baking tray.

Boil the potatoes in their skins for 15 minutes, or until just cooked. Drain, allow to cool, then peel and cut into 1 cm (½ inch) pieces.

Put the garlic, rosemary and 1 tablespoon of the oil onto a piece of foil, then twist the edges together to make a secure package. Place on the baking tray and roast for 30 minutes. Allow to cool, then squeeze the garlic from its skin and roughly chop.

Add the garlic to the potato, along with the rosemary and any oil left in the foil package. Add the remaining oil, the feta and lemon zest. Gently toss together to combine well. Season well with freshly ground black pepper and a little sea salt.

Divide the pastry in half. Roll out each half to a 3 mm (⅛ inch) thickness, then cut into a total of eight 15 cm (6 inch) rounds. Put 2 tablespoons of filling on one half of a pastry round. Combine the egg yolk and milk in a small bowl and lightly brush the unfilled half of the pastry with the egg mix. Fold over the pastry to enclose the filling, pressing gently to seal well. Crimp the edge with your fingers, or gently press with the tines of a fork. Repeat with the remaining filling and pastry rounds.

Place the pasties onto the tray, brush the tops with the remaining egg mix, then put the tray in the refrigerator for at least 30 minutes. Remove and bake for 30 minutes, or until golden. Allow the pasties to cool a little before serving, as the filling will be steaming hot.

poppy seed and parmesan filo rolls

makes 30

125 g (4^1/2 oz/1^1/4 cups) grated **parmesan cheese**

35 g (1^1/4 oz/^{1}/3 cup) **dry breadcrumbs**

2^1/2 tablespoons **poppy seeds**

2 **egg yolks**, lightly beaten

5 sheets **filo pastry**

80 g (2^3/4 oz) **butter**, melted

Preheat the oven to 180°C (350°F/Gas 4). Lightly grease a baking tray.

Combine the parmesan, breadcrumbs and poppy seeds in a bowl and season with freshly ground black pepper. Add the egg yolks, then, using a fork, work the yolks into the parmesan mixture until the mixture begins to clump together.

Place a sheet of filo pastry on the work surface, leaving the remaining sheets under a dampened tea towel (dish towel). Brush the pastry with some of the butter, then fold in half lengthways. Brush the pastry with the butter again, then sprinkle evenly with 45 g (1^1/2 oz/^{1}/3 cup slightly heaped) of parmesan mixture. Roll up the pastry as tightly as possible to form a long, thin log. Cut the log evenly into six rolls, then place the rolls, seam side down, on the baking tray. Repeat with the remaining pastry and filling mixture.

Brush the rolls with melted butter, then bake for 20 minutes, or until golden and crisp. Cool slightly, then serve warm or at room temperature, with drinks.

tomato, goat's cheese and caramelized onion flan

serves 6

1 quantity **shortcrust pastry** (page 264)

2 tablespoons **olive oil**

3 **onions**, peeled and thinly sliced

60 g (2¹/4 oz) **goat's cheese**

3 **roma (plum) tomatoes**, cut into 5 mm (1/4 inch) thick slices

1/2 teaspoon **thyme**

6 **egg yolks**

2 **eggs**, lightly beaten

250 ml (9 fl oz/1 cup) **pouring cream**

Lightly grease a 25 cm (10 inch) loose-based round tart tin.

Roll out the pastry on a lightly floured work surface until 3 mm (1/8 inch) thick, to fit the base and side of the tin. Roll the pastry around the rolling pin, then lift and ease it into the tin, gently pressing to fit the side. Trim the edges, cover with plastic wrap and refrigerate for 30 minutes. Preheat the oven to 200°C (400°F/Gas 6).

Line the pastry shell with a crumpled piece of baking paper and cover the base with baking beads or uncooked rice. Bake the pastry for 20 minutes, then remove the paper and beads and bake for a further 10 minutes, or until the pastry is golden. Remove the pastry from the oven, then reduce the oven to 160°C (315°F/Gas 2–3).

Heat the olive oil in a large, heavy-based frying pan and add the onions. Cover and cook over low heat for 30 minutes, stirring often. The onions should be reduced in volume and golden in colour.

Spread the onions evenly over the pastry shell, crumble the goat's cheese over the onions, top with the tomato slices and sprinkle with the thyme. Whisk the egg yolks, eggs and cream in a bowl until smooth, season with salt and pepper, then pour over the tomato filling. Bake for 30–40 minutes, or until the filling has just set. Allow to cool slightly before serving, either warm or at room temperature.

tip You could make this flan using blue cheese instead of goat's cheese, and some sage instead of the thyme and rosemary.

Crumble the **goat's cheese** over the onions, then arrange the **tomato** on top.

Pour **the egg** and cream **mixture** over the filling.

italian easter pie

serves 8

2 quantities **shortcrust pastry**
(page 264)

1 tablespoon **olive oil**

100 g (3¹/2 oz) **Italian-style pork sausage**, skin removed

1 **garlic clove**, chopped

1/4 teaspoon **chilli flakes**

3 **eggs**, lightly beaten

500 g (1 lb 2 oz) **fresh ricotta cheese**

50 g (1³/4 oz) **provolone cheese**, grated

30 g (1 oz) **parmesan cheese**, finely grated

80 g (2³/4 oz) **mozzarella cheese**, grated

100 g (3¹/2 oz) **prosciutto**, thinly sliced

100 g (3¹/2 oz) **mortadella**, thinly sliced

2 tablespoons finely chopped **flat-leaf (Italian) parsley**

1 **egg yolk**

1 tablespoon **milk**

Preheat the oven to 180°C (350°F/Gas 4). Lightly grease a 24 cm (9¹/2 inch) round spring-form cake tin.

Using two-thirds of the pastry, roll it out on a lightly floured work surface until 3 mm (1/8 inch) thick, to fit the base and side of the tin. Roll the pastry around the rolling pin, then lift and ease it into the tin, gently pressing to fit the side. Cover with plastic wrap and refrigerate for 30 minutes. Roll out the remaining pastry until 3 mm (1/8 inch) thick, to fit the top of the tin. Put the pastry on a large plate, cover with plastic wrap and chill for 20 minutes.

Line the pastry shell with a crumpled piece of baking paper and cover the base with baking beads or uncooked rice. Bake the pastry for 10 minutes, then remove the paper and beads and bake for a further 20 minutes, or until the pastry is golden.

Heat the olive oil in a small frying pan over medium heat, add the sausage meat, garlic and chilli flakes and cook for 5 minutes, stirring to break up the meat. Set aside to cool. Combine the cooled sausage mixture, eggs, ricotta, provolone, parmesan, mozzarella, prosciutto, mortadella and parsley in a bowl. Spoon into the pastry shell.

Combine the egg yolk with the milk and lightly brush the mixture over the edge of the pastry. Cover with the pastry round and gently press the edges to seal. Cut a small hole in the centre to allow steam to escape and brush the top with remaining egg mixture. Bake for 45 minutes, or until the pastry is golden. Cool before serving.

roasted pumpkin, garlic and pecorino pie

serves 6–8

olive oil pastry

375 g (13 oz/3 cups) **plain (all-purpose) flour**

1 teaspoon **sea salt**

125 ml (4 fl oz/1/2 cup) **extra virgin olive oil**

1 **egg**, lightly beaten

roasted pumpkin filling

1.5 kg (3 lb 5 oz) **jap (kent) pumpkin**, peeled, seeded and cut into
2 cm (3/4 inch) pieces

6 **garlic cloves**

60 ml (2 fl oz/1/4 cup) **extra virgin olive oil**

3 **eggs**, lightly beaten

100 g (31/2 oz/1 cup) grated **pecorino cheese**

2 teaspoons chopped **marjoram**

1/2 teaspoon freshly **grated nutmeg**

sea salt

bake it

Use a fork to mash the roasted
garlic and **pumpkin**.

Lay the pastry strips
diagonally across the
top of the **pie**.

318

To make the olive oil pastry, combine the flour and sea salt in a large bowl and make a well in the centre. Combine the olive oil, egg and 80 ml (2½ fl oz/⅓ cup) cold water in a small bowl and whisk to mix well. Pour the oil mixture into the well in the flour mixture, then, using a fork, stir to combine and to form a coarse dough. Add 1–2 tablespoons extra water, if necessary. Turn out the dough onto the work surface, then knead for 3 minutes, or until smooth. Wrap the dough in plastic wrap and refrigerate for 2 hours.

Preheat the oven to 200°C (400°F/Gas 6). To make the roasted pumpkin filling, put the pumpkin and unpeeled garlic cloves in a large roasting tin, drizzle with olive oil and toss to coat. Roast for 30 minutes, or until the pumpkin and garlic are tender. Cool slightly, then, when cool enough to handle, squeeze the garlic from the skins. Using a fork, mash the garlic and pumpkin, then stir in the eggs, pecorino, marjoram and nutmeg. Season with sea salt and freshly ground black pepper.

Reduce the oven to 190°C (375°F/Gas 5). Grease a 16 x 26 cm (6¼ x 10½ inch) rectangular shallow tin.

Using two-thirds of the pastry, roll out on a floured work surface to 2 mm (1/16 inch) thick, to fit the base and side of the tin; the pastry will not cover the sides all the way to the top. Cover with plastic wrap and refrigerate for 30 minutes. Spoon in the filling, smoothing it even.

Roll out the remaining pastry on a floured surface, and cut into 2 cm (3/4 inch) wide strips, long enough to fit diagonally across the pie. Position the pastry strips across the top of the pie, spacing them 1 cm (1/2 inch) apart, and trim the ends to neaten.

Bake for 1 hour, or until the pastry is crisp and golden. Serve the pie warm or at room temperature.

baked custard tarts with rhubarb

makes 8

2 quantities **sweet shortcrust pastry** (page 267)

1/2 **vanilla bean** or 1/2 teaspoon **natural vanilla extract**

250 ml (9 fl oz/1 cup) **milk**

250 ml (9 fl oz/1 cup) **pouring cream**

4 **eggs**

145 g (51/2 oz/2/3 cup) **caster (superfine) sugar**

400 g (14 oz) **rhubarb**, trimmed, then cut into 2 cm (3/4 inch) pieces

80 g (23/4 oz/1/3 cup) **soft brown sugar**

1/2 teaspoon **ground cinnamon**

1 teaspoon **lemon juice**

Preheat the oven to 200°C (400°F/Gas 6). Lightly grease eight loose-based tartlet tins, 10 cm (4 inches) in diameter and 3 cm (11/4 inches) deep.

Roll out the pastry on a lightly floured work surface to 3 mm (1/8 inch) thick. Cut the pastry into rounds to fit the base and sides of the tins. Gently press in the sides to fit, trim the edges, then cover with plastic wrap and refrigerate for 30 minutes.

Line each of the pastry shells with a crumpled piece of baking paper and fill with baking beads or uncooked rice. Bake the pastry for 15 minutes, then remove the paper and beads and bake for 7–8 minutes, or until the pastry is golden.

Reduce the oven to 160°C (315°F/Gas 2–3). If using the vanilla bean, split it down the middle and scrape out the seeds. Combine the milk, cream, vanilla bean and seeds (or vanilla extract) in a saucepan, then bring just to the boil. Whisk the eggs and sugar in a bowl until thick and pale. Pour the milk mixture onto the egg mixture, whisking to combine well. Cool the custard, then strain into a bowl. Pour the custard into the tartlet shells and bake for 25–30 minutes, or until the filling has just set. Remove from the oven.

Increase the oven to 180°C (350°F/Gas 4). Put the rhubarb, brown sugar, cinnamon, lemon juice and 2 teaspoons water in a small baking dish, toss to combine, then cover with foil and bake for 30 minutes. Remove the tartlets from the tins and just before serving spoon on the rhubarb and juices. Serve warm or at room temperature.

320

fig shortcake

serves 12

185 g (6¹/2 oz/1¹/2 cups) **plain (all-purpose) flour**

60 g (2¹/4 oz/¹/2 cup) **self-raising flour**

2 teaspoons **ground cinnamon**

1 teaspoon **ground ginger**

1 teaspoon **mixed (pumpkin pie) spice**

115 g (4 oz/¹/2 cup) **soft brown sugar**

55 g (2 oz/¹/2 cup) **ground hazelnuts**

125 g (4¹/2 oz) **unsalted butter,** chopped

1 **egg,** lightly beaten

315 g (11¹/4 oz/1 cup) **fig jam**

95 g (3¹/2 oz/2/3 cup) **hazelnuts,** toasted and finely chopped (see tip, page 76)

icing (confectioners') sugar, for dusting (optional)

Preheat the oven to 180°C (350°F/Gas 4). Grease a 35 x 11 cm (14 x 4¹/4 inch) loose-based rectangular shallow tart tin.

Combine the flours, spices, sugar and ground hazelnuts in a food processor and process to just combine. Add the butter and, using the pulse button, process in short bursts until crumbly. Add the egg, a little at a time, until the mixture comes together; you may not need all the egg. Divide the dough in half, wrap separately in plastic wrap and refrigerate for 30 minutes.

Remove one ball of dough from the refrigerator and roll out between two sheets of baking paper, large enough to fit the base and sides of the tin. Line the tin, gently pressing to fit into the corners, and patching any holes with extra dough, if necessary. Trim away the excess.

Spread the pastry with the fig jam. Using the second chilled ball of dough, coarsely grate it into a bowl, add the chopped hazelnuts and gently toss to combine. Press the mixture gently over the top of the jam, taking care to retain the grated texture. Bake for 35 minutes, or until golden brown. Cool completely in the tin before cutting, and dust lightly with icing sugar to serve, if desired. Serve with whipped cream, if desired.

The fig shortcake will keep, stored in an airtight container, for up to 4 days, or up to 3 months in the freezer.

pistachio pithiviers

serves 10

120 g (41/4 oz) **butter**, softened

145 g (51/2 oz/2/3 cup) **caster (superfine) sugar**

2 **egg yolks**

200 g (7 oz/11/3 cups) **pistachios**, lightly toasted, then finely ground (see tip, page 327)

1/2 teaspoon **natural vanilla extract**

30 g (1 oz/1/4 cup) **plain (all-purpose) flour**

2 sheets frozen **butter puff pastry**, thawed

1 **egg yolk**, extra

1 tablespoon **milk**

2 tablespoons **apricot jam**

1 tablespoon chopped **toasted pistachios**

Spoon the pistachio mixture into the middle of **one puff pastry** round.

Top **with the** second round and use your fingers **to seal** the edges.

Preheat the oven to 180°C (350°F/Gas 4). Line a baking tray with baking paper.

Cream the butter and sugar in a bowl using electric beaters until pale and fluffy, then add the yolks one at a time, beating well after each addition. Stir in the ground pistachios, vanilla and flour.

Cut the puff pastry into two 24 cm (9 1/2 inch) rounds. Place one round onto the prepared baking tray. Spoon the pistachio mixture into the middle of the pastry, smoothing the surface, leaving a 4 cm (1 1/2 inch) border around the edge. Combine the extra egg yolk and milk in a small bowl. Lightly brush around the border with the egg mixture, then top with the remaining pastry round to cover. Press the edges together to seal, then use your fingertips to crimp the edge at 2 cm (3/4 inch) intervals. Using the back of a small knife, score the pastry into wedges, starting from the centre and working out towards the edge (be careful not to cut all the way through the pastry). Brush the surface with the remaining egg mixture. Bake on the bottom shelf of the oven for 45 minutes, or until golden and puffed.

Heat the jam in a small saucepan with 1 tablespoon water. As soon as the pithiviers comes out of the oven, brush liberally with the apricot glaze, then sprinkle with the chopped pistachios. Allow to cool, then serve.

The pithiviers is best eaten the day it is made.

tip Toasted nuts can be ground in a food processor. Place the cooled nuts in the bowl and, using the pulse button, process in short bursts until the nuts resemble breadcrumbs; do not overprocess or the nuts will become oily. If the recipe uses sugar, it helps to add a little to the nuts when processing to help absorb some of the oil. Small quantities of nuts can be ground in a clean coffee grinder.

peach galettes

makes 12

2 quantities **sweet shortcrust pastry** (page 267)

600 g (1 lb 5 oz) **peaches**, stoned and thinly sliced

20 g (3/4 oz) **butter**, melted

1 tablespoon **honey**

1 tablespoon **caster (superfine) sugar**

1/4 teaspoon **ground nutmeg**

1 **egg yolk**

1 tablespoon **milk**

3 tablespoons **apricot jam**

25 g (1 oz/1/4 cup) **flaked almonds**, toasted

Lightly grease a baking tray or line it with baking paper.

Roll out the pastry on a lightly floured work surface to 3 mm (1/8 inch) thick. Cut out twelve 12 cm (41/2 inch) rounds. Gently toss together the peach slices, butter, honey, sugar and nutmeg in a bowl. Divide the peach mixture between the pastry rounds, leaving a 1 cm (1/2 inch) border around the edge. Fold the pastry over the filling, leaving the centre uncovered, pleating the pastry at 1 cm (1/2 inch) intervals to fit. Place the galettes on the tray and refrigerate for 30 minutes. Meanwhile, preheat the oven to 200°C (400°F/Gas 6).

Combine the egg yolk and milk in a small bowl to make a glaze. Brush the glaze over the edges of the pastry. Bake for 30 minutes, or until golden.

Combine the apricot jam and 1 tablespoon water in a small saucepan and stir over low heat until smooth. Brush the jam mixture over the hot galettes, then sprinkle with almonds. Cool before serving.

cocoa and date crostata

serves 12

500 g (1 lb 2 oz/2³/4 cups) **pitted dried dates**

1/2 teaspoon **natural vanilla extract**

2 teaspoons **lemon zest**

1/2 teaspoon **ground cinnamon**

1/2 teaspoon **ground ginger**

30 g (1 oz/1/4 cup) **unsweetened cocoa powder**

1 tablespoon **soft brown sugar**

1/4 teaspoon **bicarbonate of soda (baking soda)**

1 1/2 quantities **sweet shortcrust pastry** (page 267), but substitute 75 g (2¹/2 oz) **toasted walnuts**, blended until fine, for 75 g (2¹/2 oz) of the flour

1 **egg yolk**

1 teaspoon **caster (superfine) sugar**

1/4 teaspoon **ground cinnamon**, extra

Preheat the oven to 180°C (350°F/Gas 4). Put the dates, vanilla, lemon zest, cinnamon, ginger, cocoa powder, brown sugar and 250 ml (9 fl oz/1 cup) water in a heavy-based saucepan over medium heat. Bring to a simmer, then add the bicarbonate of soda, stir to combine and set aside to cool. Transfer the mixture to a food processor and, using the pulse button, mix to form a coarse paste.

Grease a deep, 25 cm (10 inch) loose-based round tart tin. Using two-thirds of the pastry, roll out the pastry to fit the base and side of the tin. Roll out the remaining pastry to form a round, large enough for the top.

Spoon the filling over the pastry, smoothing the top. Combine the egg yolk with 1 tablespoon water and brush the edges with the egg wash. Place the pastry round over the date filling, gently pressing to remove any air bubbles, and pressing the edges of the pastry together to seal. Cut a slit in the middle of the pastry to allow the steam to escape, then brush the top with the remaining egg wash. Sprinkle with the cinnamon mix.

Place on the bottom shelf of the oven and bake for 1 hour, or until golden. Cool completely before serving.

baked desserts

about baked desserts

Dessert is a luxury, a sweet indulgence that signals the end of a meal. However, desserts, or puddings, weren't always the sweet dishes we enjoy today. In the Middle Ages puddings made from a mixture of grain and dried fruit were assembled in a thick cloth (or animal gut) and cooked in large pans of boiling water. The blancmange of medieval England was a thick gruel made with almonds, milk, rice and chicken, and has evolved to become a sweet custard thickened with gelatine and set in moulds. Although cane syrup, honey and fruit have been used as sweeteners for thousands of years, sugar only reached the Western world in the 14th century. Then, sugar was called white gold as it was very expensive. It was used in medicines, to cover the bitter taste, and was the domain of only the very wealthy, who sprinkled it on just about everything. By the 18th century, sugar became more plentiful, prices dropped, and sugar became readily available to all — and so the sweet dessert was born.

baked desserts today

Today there are hundreds of different types of desserts that we bake for friends and family to share; for any occasion, both formal and fun. These dishes are often made using a traditional baking method — whisking eggs for a soufflé, creaming butter and sugar for a sponge pudding, or making pastry for a cheesecake crust. Desserts are enjoyed the world over — different cultures have their own versions of desserts yet it is surprising how similar they can be. Sweet rice puddings come in many forms, from India, Greece and Italy, to the sticky black rice puddings eaten in Thailand.

What is it that makes a baked dessert so tempting? Our anticipation as we smell the glorious aromas wafting from the oven as they bake. Or perhaps it's the childhood memories evoked by the mouthwatering aromas and sweet scents? Desserts are those dishes we all love to bake; they allow our creativity to shine. Desserts are dishes we crave on colder days, both comforting and familiar. They are a treat for some and a daily enjoyment for others.

hints and tips

- Always read the recipe through before you start cooking and make sure you have all the ingredients ready and the correct equipment necessary. Preheat the oven.

- Have the baking dish, or dishes, greased and lined (as necessary) before you start.

- Measure a dish using its liquid capacity.

- If using butter to grease a baking dish, first melt in a small saucepan over a low heat or in the microwave on medium for 30 seconds. Use a pastry brush to brush thoroughly and evenly over the inside of the dish.

- If using ready-made frozen pastry, allow it to thaw completely before use.

- If whisking egg whites, make sure you use clean beaters and a clean, dry bowl or the whites will not whisk to their full volume.

- When a recipe requires a dish to be baked in a roasting tin filled with boiling water, make sure the kettle is filled, boiled and ready to pour as soon as it is needed. You may prefer to fill the dish with boiling water once the roasting tin is sitting on the oven tray. This will prevent you from having to carefully carry a tray filled with boiling water to the oven.

- Always use oven gloves when transferring a tin filled with boiling water: the tin may not be hot but the water is.

- When baking a soufflé, never open the oven door until the cooking time is reached.

- Always use oven gloves when unmoulding a hot pudding.

mixed berry sponge puddings

serves 6

1 tablespoon **melted unsalted butter**

125 g (4¹/2 oz) **unsalted butter**, softened

115 g (4 oz/¹/2 cup) **caster (superfine) sugar**, plus 6 teaspoons extra

2 **eggs**

165 g (5³/4 oz/1¹/3 cups) **self-raising flour**, sifted

60 ml (2 fl oz/¹/4 cup) **milk**

200 g (7 oz) **mixed berries**, fresh or frozen

Preheat the oven to 180°C (350°F/Gas 4). Grease six 125 ml (4 fl oz/¹/2 cup) pudding or dariole moulds with melted butter.

Cream the butter and sugar in a bowl using electric beaters until pale and fluffy. Add the eggs one at a time, beating well after each addition. Gently fold in the flour alternately with the milk.

Divide the berries between the moulds and top each with a teaspoon of the extra caster sugar. Top the berries with the pudding mixture, dividing the mixture evenly between the moulds.

Put the puddings in a large roasting tin and pour in enough hot water to come halfway up the sides of the moulds. Cover the baking tin with a sheet of baking paper, then cover with foil, pleating two sheets of foil together if necessary. Fold the foil tightly around the edges of the tin to seal.

Bake the puddings for 35–40 minutes, or until the pudding springs back when touched. Remove the puddings from the water bath, leave to cool in the moulds for 5 minutes, then run a small knife around the inside of the mould and turn out onto plates. Serve with custard or ice cream.

bake it

banana and plum crumble

serves 4–6

30 g (1 oz/1/4 cup) **plain (all-purpose) flour**

50 g (13/4 oz/1/2 cup) **rolled oats**

30 g (1 oz/1/2 cup) **shredded coconut**

45 g (13/4 oz/1/4 cup) lightly packed **soft brown sugar**

finely grated **zest** from 1 **lime**

100 g (31/2 oz) **unsalted butter**, cut into cubes

2 **bananas**, peeled and halved lengthways

4 **plums**, halved and stoned

60 ml (2 fl oz/1/4 cup) **lime juice**

Preheat the oven to 180°C (350°F/Gas 4). Combine the flour, rolled oats, coconut, sugar and zest in a small bowl. Add the butter and, using your fingertips, rub the butter into the flour mixture until crumbly.

Put the bananas and plums in a 1.25 litre (44 fl oz/5 cup) capacity ovenproof dish and pour over the lime juice. Toss to coat in the juice. Sprinkle the crumble mixture evenly over the fruit. Bake for 25–30 minutes, or until the crumble is golden. Serve hot with ice cream or whipped cream.

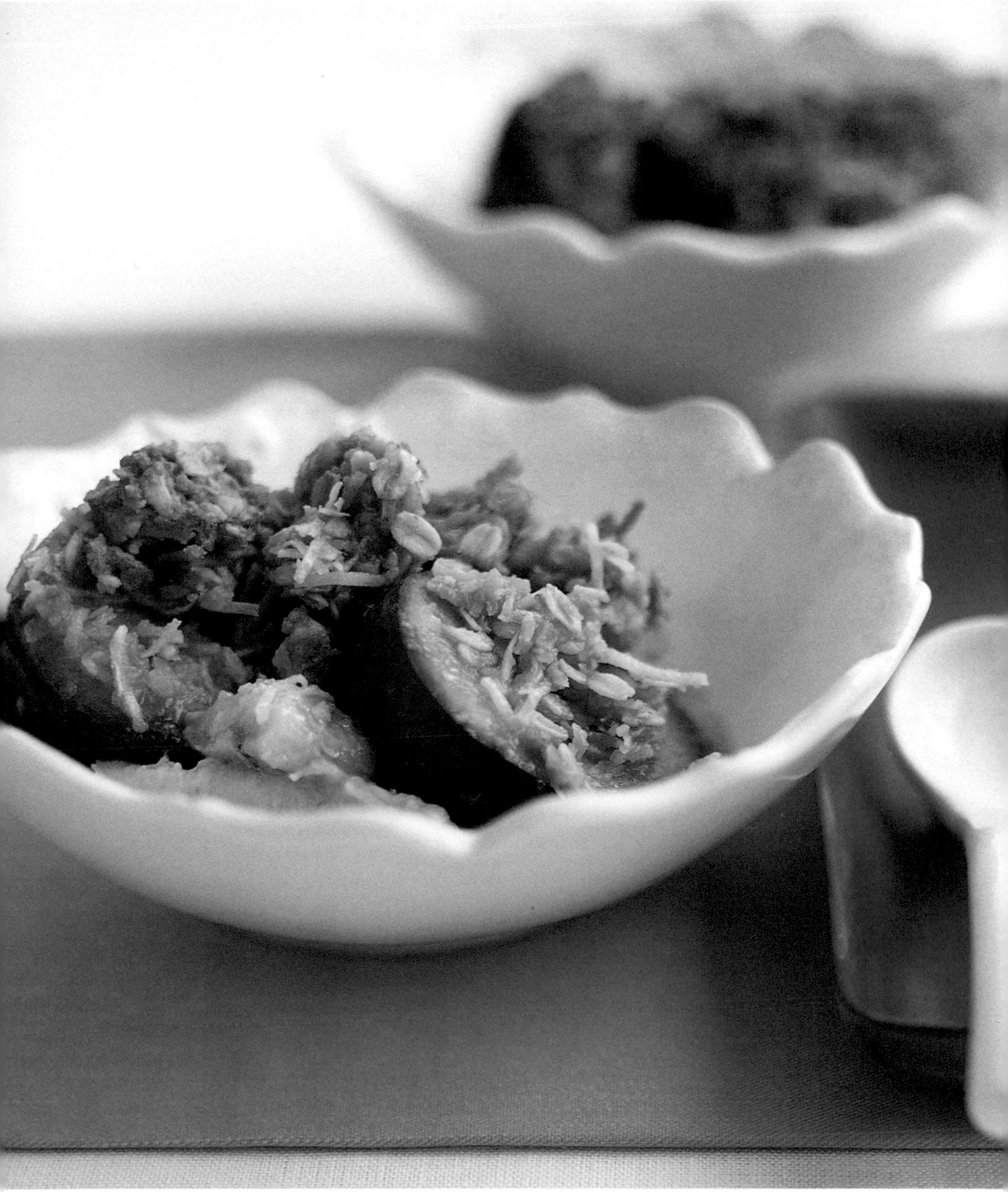

pear dumplings

serves 6

6 firm, ripe **pears**

100 g (3¹/2 oz) **goat's cheese**, crumbled

55 g (2 oz/¹/2 cup) **ground almonds**

¹/2 teaspoon **ground nutmeg**

¹/2 teaspoon **grated lemon zest**

55 g (2 oz/¹/4 cup) **caster (superfine) sugar**

1¹/2 quantities **sweet shortcrust pastry** (page 267)

1 **egg**, lightly beaten

icing (confectioners') sugar, for dusting

crème anglaise, to serve (page 385)

Preheat the oven to 180°C (350°F/Gas 4). Grease a large roasting tin.

Leaving the pears whole and unpeeled, core the pears using an apple corer. Combine the goat's cheese, almonds, nutmeg, lemon zest and 2 tablespoons of the sugar. Using a teaspoon, fill the pear cavities with the goat's cheese mixture.

Roll out the pastry to 3 mm (¹/8 inch) thick and cut into six 15 cm (6 inch) squares. Lightly brush the squares with egg and sprinkle with the remaining sugar. Place a pear in the centre of each piece of pastry and bring the corners of the pastry up and around the pear to completely enclose it. Press the edges together to seal, trimming where necessary, and reserving the pastry scraps.

Using a small knife, cut 12 leaf shapes from the pastry scraps. Brush the dumplings with the remaining egg and attach two pastry leaves to the top of each, pressing firmly to secure. Transfer to the roasting tin and bake for 35–40 minutes, or until the pastry is golden and the pears are tender. Dust with icing sugar and serve immediately with crème anglaise.

chocolate mint self-saucing pudding

serves 6

185 ml (6 fl oz/3/4 cup) **milk**

115 g (4 oz/1/2 cup) **caster (superfine) sugar**

60 g (21/4 oz) **unsalted butter**, melted

1 **egg**

125 g (41/2 oz/1 cup) **self-raising flour**

40 g (11/2 oz/1/3 cup) **unsweetened cocoa powder**

125 g (41/2 oz) **dark mint-flavoured chocolate**, roughly chopped

230 g (8 oz/1 cup) **soft brown sugar**

ice cream, to serve

Preheat the oven to 180°C (350°F/Gas 4). Grease a 1.5 litre (52 fl oz/6 cup) capacity ovenproof dish.

Whisk together the milk, sugar, butter and egg in a bowl. Sift the flour and half the cocoa powder onto the milk mixture, add the chocolate and stir to mix well. Pour the mixture into the dish. Put the brown sugar and remaining cocoa powder into a bowl and stir in 250 ml (9 fl oz/1 cup) boiling water. Carefully pour this over the pudding mixture.

Bake for 40–45 minutes, or until the pudding is cooked and is firm to the touch. Spoon over the sauce and serve hot or warm with ice cream.

tip If you prefer, substitute plain dark chocolate or another type of flavoured chocolate (such as orange chocolate) for the mint chocolate.

individual panettone puddings

makes 8

200 ml (7 fl oz) **milk**

200 ml (7 fl oz) **pouring cream**

1 teaspoon **natural vanilla extract**

3 **eggs**

115 g (4 oz/1/2 cup) **caster (superfine) sugar**

150 g (51/2 oz) **panettone**

60 g (21/4 oz/1/2 cup) **sultanas (golden raisins)**

custard or **crème anglaise**, to serve (page 385)

Preheat the oven to 150°C (300°F/Gas 2). Grease eight 125 ml (4 fl oz/1/2 cup) timbale moulds with butter.

Combine the milk, cream and vanilla in a saucepan, heat until almost boiling, then remove from the heat. Whisk the eggs and sugar in a bowl until pale and thick, then gradually add the cream mixture, whisking to combine well.

Cut the panettone into 1.5 cm (5/8 inch) thick slices and then cut into rounds using a 5 cm (2 inch) cutter (you will need 16 rounds in total). Place a round in the base of each mould, sprinkle over the sultanas, then pour 60 ml (2 fl oz/1/4 cup) of the custard mixture over each. Top with another round and enough custard mixture to cover the panettone and fill the mould.

Put the puddings in a large roasting tin and pour in enough hot water to come halfway up the sides of the moulds. Bake for 25–30 minutes, or until golden and firm. Remove the moulds from the hot water and allow to cool for 5 minutes before inverting onto serving plates. Serve with the custard.

tip You could make these puddings using brioche instead of panettone.

spiced quince charlotte

serves 4–6

460 g (1 lb/2 cups) **caster (superfine) sugar**

1 **vanilla bean**

1 **cinnamon stick**

1 teaspoon **ground allspice**

1.5 kg (3 lb 5 oz) **quinces**, peeled, quartered and cored

unsalted butter

2 loaves thinly sliced **brioche**

crème anglaise, to serve (page 385)

Preheat the oven to 180°C (350°F/Gas 4).

Combine 1 litre (35 fl oz/4 cups) water and the sugar in a saucepan and stir over medium heat until the sugar dissolves. Split the vanilla bean down the middle and scrape out the seeds. Put the bean and its seeds in the saucepan with the cinnamon and allspice. Remove from the heat.

Place the quinces in a roasting tin or baking dish and pour over the syrup. Cover with foil and bake for 2 hours, or until the fruit is very tender. Drain the quinces.

Butter the slices of brioche. Cut out a circle from two slices of brioche (cut a half-circle from each slice), large enough to fit the base of a 2 litre (70 fl oz/8 cup) capacity charlotte mould or ovenproof bowl. Reserving 4 slices of brioche for the top, cut the remaining brioche into 2 cm (3/4 inch) wide fingers, and long enough to fit the height of the mould. Press the brioche vertically around the side of the dish, overlapping the strips slightly.

Put the quinces in the brioche-lined mould and cover with the reserved slices of brioche. Sit the mould on a baking tray and bake for 25–30 minutes. Allow to cool for 10 minutes, then unmould onto a serving plate. Serve with the crème anglaise.

tip Brioche is a rich, buttery bread that has an almost cake-like texture. It is available from most bakeries. If preferred, substitute with 1 loaf of sliced white bread (crusts removed).

orange and prune rice cake

serves 8

1 **vanilla bean** or 1 teaspoon **natural vanilla extract**

200 g (7 oz/1 cup) **medium-grain rice**

1 litre (35 fl oz/4 cups) **milk**

1 **fresh bay leaf**, bruised

2 1/2 teaspoons finely grated **orange zest**

4 **eggs**, lightly beaten

170 g (6 oz/3/4 cup) **caster (superfine) sugar**

200 g (7 oz) **fresh ricotta cheese**

60 g (2 1/4 oz/1/2 cup) **slivered almonds**

whipped cream, to serve

prune filling

200 g (7 oz) **pitted prunes**

115 g (4 oz/1/2 cup) **caster (superfine) sugar**

125 ml (4 fl oz/1/2 cup) **sweet Marsala**

To make the filling, put the prunes in a heatproof bowl with 625 ml (21¹/2 fl oz/ 2¹/2 cups) boiling water. Leave to soften for 30 minutes. Put the prune mixture in a saucepan with the sugar and Marsala and slowly bring to the boil. Reduce the heat to low and simmer for 15 minutes, or until the prunes are very soft. Cool the prunes in the liquid, then strain, reserving the liquid.

If using the vanilla bean, split it down the middle and scrape out the seeds, then put the bean and its seeds in a saucepan with the rice, milk and bay leaf. Bring slowly to a simmer, then cover and cook over medium–low heat for 15–20 minutes, or until the rice is tender and most of the liquid has absorbed. Set aside, covered, for 20 minutes, or until cooled slightly. Remove the bay leaf and vanilla bean.

Preheat the oven to 170°C (325°F/Gas 3). Lightly grease an 18 cm (7 inch) round spring-form cake tin and line the base with baking paper. Wrap a piece of foil tightly around the base and up the outside of the tin to completely seal it.

Combine the orange zest, eggs, sugar, ricotta (and vanilla extract, if using) in a bowl and, using a wooden spoon, stir until smooth. Add the egg mixture to the rice and stir to combine well. Pour half of the rice mixture into the prepared tin and smooth the top. Arrange the prunes on top, pour over the remaining mixture and scatter over the almonds.

Put the cake tin in a roasting tin and pour in enough boiling water to come halfway up the side of the cake tin. Bake for 50 minutes, or until the cake is firm in the centre. Cover the cake with foil halfway through cooking if it browns too quickly.

Meanwhile, put the reserved prune liquid into a small saucepan and bring to the boil. Reduce the heat to low and simmer for 15 minutes, or until the liquid has reduced by one-third. Cool the rice cake in the tin. Turn out onto a serving plate and serve with whipped cream and the syrup.

Put the prunes and water in a **saucepan** with the sugar and Marsala.

Arrange **the prunes** over the top of the rice.

sunken chocolate dessert cakes

serves 4

1 tablespoon **melted unsalted butter**

115 g (4 oz/1/2 cup) **caster (superfine) sugar**, plus 1 tablespoon extra

150 g (51/2 oz) **dark chocolate**, chopped

125 g (41/2 oz) **butter**

3 **eggs**

30 g (1 oz/1/4 cup) **plain (all-purpose) flour**

ice cream, to serve

Preheat the oven to 180°C (350°F/Gas 4). Grease four 250 ml (9 fl oz/1 cup) ramekins with the melted butter and coat lightly with the extra sugar.

Put the chocolate and butter in a small heatproof bowl. Sit the bowl over a small saucepan of simmering water, stirring frequently until the chocolate and butter have melted. Take care that the base of the bowl doesn't touch the water. Remove from the heat.

Whisk the eggs and sugar in a bowl using electric beaters until pale and thick. Sift the flour onto the egg mixture, then whisk the flour into the mixture. Whisk in the melted chocolate.

Divide the batter between the prepared ramekins and place on a baking tray. Bake for 30–35 minutes, or until set and firm to touch. Allow to cool in the ramekins for 10 minutes before turning out onto serving plates (if they are reluctant to come out, run a knife around the inside edge of the ramekins to loosen them). Alternatively, serve them in the ramekins, dusted with icing sugar. Serve warm with ice cream.

baked pears in spiced sauternes syrup

serves 6

250 ml (9 fl oz/1 cup) **Sauternes** or any **dessert wine**

345 g (12 oz/1¹/2 cups) **caster (superfine) sugar**

2 **cardamom pods**, bruised

2 **cloves**

1 **cinnamon stick**

1 **star anise**

1 teaspoon **rosewater**

1 small piece of **lemon rind**, white pith removed

6 **corella (or other small) pears**, peeled

125 ml (4 fl oz/¹/2 cup) **Greek-style yoghurt**

1 tablespoon **honey**

Preheat the oven to 180°C (350°F/Gas 4).

Combine 750 ml (26 fl oz/3 cups) water with the Sauternes, sugar, cardamom, cloves, cinnamon stick, star anise, rosewater and lemon rind in a saucepan. Stir over medium heat for 4–5 minutes, or until the sugar dissolves. Bring the mixture to the boil, then reduce the heat to low and cook for 8 minutes, or until the syrup has reduced by half.

Halve the pears, place them in a roasting tin and pour over the syrup. Cover with foil and bake for 20 minutes. Remove the foil, baste the pears with the syrup, then cook for a further 20 minutes, or until the pears are tender.

Combine the yoghurt and honey in a small bowl. Serve the pears warm or at room temperature with the yoghurt and a little syrup spooned over.

baked passionfruit cheesecake

serves 6–8

60 g (2¼ oz/½ cup) **plain (all-purpose) flour**

30 g (1 oz/¼ cup) **self-raising flour**

50 g (1¾ oz) **unsalted butter**

2 tablespoons **caster (superfine) sugar**

grated **zest** from 1 **lemon**

2 tablespoon **lemon juice**

filling

600 g (1 lb 5 oz) **cream cheese**, softened

170 g (6 oz/¾ cup) **caster (superfine) sugar**

30 g (1 oz/¼ cup) **plain (all-purpose) flour**

125 ml (4 fl oz/½ cup) **strained passionfruit juice**

4 **eggs**

170 ml (5½ fl oz/⅔ cup) **pouring cream**

Combine the flours, butter, sugar and lemon zest in a food processor. Add the lemon juice and, using the pulse button, process until a dough forms. Cover with plastic wrap and refrigerate for 1 hour.

Meanwhile, preheat the oven to 180°C (350°F/Gas 4). Grease a 22 cm (8½ inch) round spring-form cake tin.

Roll out the pastry to 5 mm (¼ inch) thick. Roll the pastry around the pin, lift and ease it into the tin, pressing to fit, then trim the edges. Refrigerate for 10 minutes. Bake for 15–20 minutes, or until golden. Remove from the oven and cool. Reduce the oven to 150°C (300°F/Gas 2).

To make the filling, beat the cream cheese and sugar using electric beaters until smooth. Add the flour and passionfruit juice and beat until combined. Add the eggs one at a time, beating well after each addition. Stir in the cream, then pour the mixture over the cooled base. Bake for 1 hour, or until the centre is just firm to the touch (move the cheesecake to the lowest shelf of the oven for the last 10 minutes of cooking and cover with foil to prevent overbrowning). Cool the cheesecake in the tin before removing and serving in slices.

tip You will need about 6 passionfruit to obtain 125 ml (4 fl oz/½ cup) passionfruit juice. Tinned passionfruit pulp is not an adequate substitute.

cardamom, orange and plum dessert cakes

makes 8

185 g (6¹/2 oz) **unsalted butter**, chopped

95 g (3¹/4 oz/1/2 cup) **soft brown sugar**

115 g (4 oz/1/2 cup) **caster (superfine) sugar**

3 **eggs**

1 teaspoon finely grated **orange zest**

310 g (11 oz/2¹/2 cups) **self-raising flour**, sifted

1 teaspoon **ground cardamom**

185 ml (6 fl oz/3/4 cup) **milk**

4 **tinned plums**, drained and patted dry, cut in half

1 tablespoon **raw (demerara) sugar**

thick (double/heavy) cream, to serve

Preheat the oven to 180°C (350°F/Gas 4). Lightly grease eight 250 ml (9 fl oz/1 cup) ceramic ramekins and dust with flour, shaking out any excess flour.

Cream the butter and sugars in a bowl using electric beaters until pale and fluffy. Add the eggs, one at a time and beating well after each addition, then stir in the orange zest. Fold the flour and cardamom into the butter mixture alternately with the milk until combined and smooth.

Divide the mixture between the ramekins and place a plum half, cut side down, on top of the batter. Sprinkle with raw sugar, place the ramekins on a baking tray and bake for 30–35 minutes, or until golden and firm to the touch. Serve warm or at room temperature with thick cream.

citrus delicious

serves 4–6

60 g (2¼ oz) **unsalted butter**, softened

170 g (6 oz/¾ cup) **caster (superfine) sugar**

3 **eggs**, separated

125 ml (4 fl oz/½ cup) **citrus juice** (see tip)

250 ml (9 fl oz/1 cup) **milk**

60 g (2¼ oz/½ cup) **self-raising flour**

2 tablespoons finely grated **citrus zest**

ice cream, to serve

Preheat the oven to 180°C (350°F/Gas 4). Grease a 1.25 litre (44 fl oz/5 cup) capacity ovenproof dish.

Cream the butter and sugar in a bowl using electric beaters until pale and fluffy. Add the egg yolks one at a time, beating well after each addition. Stir in the citrus juice, milk, flour and zest, combining well.

Whisk the egg whites in a clean, dry bowl until stiff peaks form, then gently fold into the batter. Spoon the mixture into the dish. Put the dish in a large roasting tin and pour in enough hot water to come halfway up the side of the dish. Bake for 40–45 minutes, or until golden and puffed (cover with foil if the top starts to brown too quickly). Serve hot or warm with ice cream.

tip Use a combination of oranges, lemons and limes for the juice and zest.

queen of puddings

serves 6

500 ml (17 fl oz/2 cups) **milk**

50 g (1³/4 oz) **unsalted butter**

140 g (5 oz/1³/4 cups) **fresh breadcrumbs**

115 g (4 oz/¹/2 cup) **caster (superfine) sugar**, plus 1 tablespoon extra

finely grated **zest** from 1 **orange**

5 **eggs**, separated

210 g (7¹/2 oz/2/3 cup) **orange marmalade**

1 teaspoon **honey**

whipped cream, to serve

Preheat the oven to 180°C (350°F/Gas 4). Lightly grease a 1.25 litre (44 fl oz/5 cup) rectangular ovenproof dish.

Combine the milk and butter in a small saucepan and heat over low heat until the butter has melted. Put the breadcrumbs, the extra sugar and orange zest in a large bowl. Stir in the milk mixture and set aside for 10 minutes.

Lightly whisk the egg yolks, then stir them into the breadcrumb mixture. Spoon into the prepared dish, then bake for 25–30 minutes, or until firm to touch.

Combine the marmalade and honey in a saucepan and heat over low heat until melted. Pour evenly over the pudding. Whisk the egg whites in a clean, dry bowl until stiff peaks form. Gradually add the sugar, whisking well, until the mixture is stiff and glossy and the sugar has dissolved. Spoon the meringue evenly over the top of the pudding and bake for 12–15 minutes, or until the meringue is golden. Serve the pudding warm with whipped cream.

cream cheese soufflés

makes 6

50 g (1 3/4 oz) **unsalted butter**, melted

55 g (2 oz/1/4 cup) **caster (superfine) sugar**, for dusting

250 g (9 oz) **cream cheese**

55 g (2 oz/1/4 cup) **caster (superfine) sugar**, extra

3 **eggs**, separated

2 tablespoons **plain (all-purpose) flour**

500 ml (17 fl oz/2 cups) **milk**

1 tablespoon **Grand Marnier** or **other orange liqueur**

finely grated **zest** from 1 **orange**

icing (confectioners') sugar, for dusting

3 **oranges**, peeled and segmented, to serve

Preheat the oven to 200°C (400°F/Gas 6). Grease six 250 ml (9 fl oz/1 cup) soufflé dishes with the melted butter and dust with the sugar.

Combine the cream cheese, extra sugar and egg yolks in a heatproof bowl and beat using electric beaters until very smooth. Stir in the flour. Combine the milk, Grand Marnier and orange zest in a saucepan and bring almost to boiling point. Whisk the milk mixture into the cream cheese mixture, stir until smooth, then return to a clean saucepan. Stir constantly over very low heat for 5–7 minutes, or until the custard thickens slightly; do not allow the custard to boil.

Whisk the egg whites in a clean, dry bowl until stiff peaks form, then gently fold into the warm custard mixture. Place the prepared soufflé dishes on an oven tray. Fill the dishes two-thirds full with the soufflé mixture. Cook for 15 minutes, or until the soufflés are well risen and firm to the touch.

Serve immediately dusted with icing sugar and with the orange segments.

tip When dusting the soufflé dish with sugar, turn the dish so the sugar coats the entire surface of the dish, then turn the dish upside down and tap out any excess. The sugar helps the soufflé to 'grip' and climb up the side of the dish as it cooks.

Use a pastry brush to lightly **grease** the soufflé dishes with **butter**.

Fill the **soufflé dish** to three-quarters full with the **cream** cheese mixture.

prune and almond clafoutis

serves 6

250 ml (9 fl oz/1 cup) **pouring cream**

100 ml (3¹/2 fl oz) **milk**

1 teaspoon **natural vanilla extract**

3 **eggs**

80 g (2³/4 oz/¹/3 cup) **caster (superfine) sugar**

80 g (2³/4 oz/³/4 cup) **ground almonds**

340 g (12 oz) **pitted prunes**

icing (confectioners') sugar, for dusting

custard or **crème anglaise**, to serve (page 385)

whipped cream, to serve (optional)

Preheat the oven to 180°C (350°F/Gas 4). Lightly grease a shallow 750 ml (26 fl oz/ 3 cup) capacity ovenproof dish.

Combine the cream, milk and vanilla in a saucepan. Bring to a simmer over low heat, then remove from the heat and cool slightly.

Whisk together the eggs, sugar and ground almonds in a bowl. Add the cream mixture and stir to combine well. Scatter the prunes over the prepared dish. Pour the batter over the prunes and bake for 35–40 minutes, or until golden. Dust with icing sugar, pour over the custard and serve with whipped cream, if desired.

semolina pudding with saffron apricots

serves 8–10

1 litre (35 fl oz/4 cups) **milk**

230 g (8 oz/1 cup) **caster (superfine) sugar**

1 **cinnamon stick**

1 **vanilla bean** or 1 teaspoon **natural vanilla extract**

125 g (4¹/2 oz/1 cup) **semolina**

50 g (1³/4 oz) **unsalted butter**, cubed

5 **eggs**, separated

250 ml (9 fl oz/1 cup) **orange juice**

80 g (2³/4 oz/¹/3 cup) **caster (superfine) sugar**, extra

1 **star anise**

a pinch of **saffron threads**

200 g (7 oz) **dried apricot halves**

Preheat the oven to 180°C (350°F/Gas 4). Grease a 2 litre (70 fl oz/8 cup) capacity ovenproof dish.

Combine the milk, sugar and cinnamon stick in a large saucepan. If using the vanilla bean, split it down the middle and scrape out the seeds, then add the bean and its seeds to the pan. Stir over medium heat until the sugar has dissolved; do not allow to boil. Gradually sprinkle the semolina over the hot milk mixture, then, stirring continuously, bring to a simmer and cook for 8–10 minutes, or until the mixture has thickened. Remove from the heat and discard the cinnamon and vanilla bean. Stir in the butter (and the vanilla extract, if using). Remove about 130 g (4¹/2 oz/¹/2 cup) of the semolina mixture to a bowl, add the egg yolks and whisk together. Return the egg and semolina mixture to the saucepan, stirring to mix well.

Whisk the egg whites in a clean, dry bowl until stiff peaks form, then gently fold into the semolina mixture. Pour the mixture into the prepared dish. Put the pudding in a large roasting tin and pour in enough hot water to come halfway up the side of the dish. Bake for 55–60 minutes, or until the pudding is set and golden.

Meanwhile, combine the orange juice, extra sugar, star anise, saffron and 125 ml (4 fl oz/¹/2 cup) water in a small saucepan. Bring to the boil, then reduce the heat and simmer for 10 minutes. Add the apricots and continue to simmer over very low heat for a further 10–12 minutes, or until the apricots are soft and tender. Remove from the heat and discard the star anise. Spoon the pudding into serving bowls and serve hot or warm with the apricots.

maple syrup rice puddings

serves 6

110 g (3³/4 oz/¹/2 cup) **short-grain rice**

750 ml (26 fl oz/3 cups) **milk**

115 g (4 oz/¹/2 cup) **caster (superfine) sugar**

1 teaspoon **natural vanilla extract**

125 ml (4 fl oz/¹/2 cup) **thick (double/heavy) cream**

60 ml (2 fl oz/¹/4 cup) **maple syrup**

115 g (4 oz/¹/2 cup) firmly packed **soft brown sugar**

pouring cream, to serve (optional)

Preheat the oven to 180°C (350°F/Gas 4). Lightly grease six 125 ml (4 fl oz/¹/2 cup) pudding or dariole moulds with butter.

Combine the rice, milk, sugar and vanilla in a large saucepan and stir to mix well. Bring to the boil, then reduce the heat to low and simmer for 25–30 minutes, stirring often, or until the rice is tender. Remove from the heat, stir in the cream and set aside for 10 minutes.

Spoon 2 teaspoons of maple syrup and 1 tablespoon of the brown sugar into each mould. Top with the rice mixture and bake for 30 minutes, or until set and golden. Rest in the moulds for 15 minutes, then turn out onto plates and serve with cream, if desired.

ricotta and cream cheese pudding

serves 6–8

250 g (9 oz) **cream cheese**

125 g (4¹/2 oz) **fresh ricotta cheese**

115 g (4 oz/¹/2 cup) **caster (superfine) sugar**

125 ml (4 fl oz/¹/2 cup) **thick (double/heavy) cream**

1 tablespoon **warm honey**

1 teaspoon **natural vanilla extract**

5 **eggs**, separated

30 g (1 oz/¹/4 cup) **sultanas (golden raisins)**

35 g (1¹/4 oz/¹/4 cup) chopped **toasted pistachios**

grated **zest** and **juice** from 1 **lemon**

fresh berries and **pouring cream**, to serve

Preheat the oven to 180°C (350°F/Gas 4). Grease a 2 litre (70 fl oz/8 cup) capacity ovenproof dish.

Combine the cream cheese, ricotta and sugar in a large bowl and beat with electric beaters until smooth. Add the cream, honey and vanilla and beat well. Add the egg yolks one at a time, beating well after each addition. Stir in the sultanas, nuts, lemon zest and juice.

Whisk the egg whites in a clean, dry bowl until stiff peaks form, then gently fold into the pudding mixture. Pour into the prepared dish. Put the dish in a large roasting tin and pour in enough hot water to come halfway up the side of the dish. Cover the roasting tin with baking paper, then cover with foil, tightly folding the foil around the edges of the tin to seal. Bake for 50–55 minutes, or until the pudding has set and is puffed and firm. Serve with fresh berries and cream.

baked almond and marzipan peaches

serves 6

3 large ripe, firm **peaches**

40 g (1 1/2 oz/1/3 cup) roughly chopped **dark chocolate**

50 g (1 3/4 oz/1/3 cup) **whole blanched almonds**, toasted and chopped

2 1/2 tablespoons **marzipan**, chopped

2 tablespoons **caster (superfine) sugar**

1 1/2 tablespoons **unsalted butter**, softened

1 **egg yolk**, lightly beaten

thick (double/heavy) cream or **crème anglaise**, to serve (page 385)

Preheat the oven to 170°C (325°F/Gas 3). Lightly grease a roasting tin or large ceramic ovenproof dish.

Cut the peaches in half on either side of the stone. Remove any remaining flesh from the stone and finely chop, then combine in a bowl with the remaining ingredients, stirring to combine.

Place the peaches, skin side down, in the tin. Divide the stuffing mixture among the peaches, pressing the mixture firmly onto the peach, heaping the mixture slightly if necessary. Bake the peaches for 30 minutes, or until the peaches have softened and the filling is bubbling. Cool slightly, then serve warm or at room temperature with thick cream or crème anglaise.

tip Peaches can be either clingstone (the flesh clings to the stone), as used for this recipe, or slipstone (the flesh separates easily from the stone). If you are using slipstone peaches, you will find you can easily cut the peach in half through the middle.

baked chocolate custards

serves 10

30 g (1 oz) **unsalted butter**, melted

55 g (2 oz/1/4 cup) **caster (superfine) sugar**, for dusting

300 ml (101/2 fl oz) **pouring cream**

200 ml (7 fl oz) **milk**

200 g (7 oz) **dark chocolate**, roughly chopped

grated **zest** from 1 **orange**

6 **eggs**

115 g (4 oz/1/2 cup) **caster (superfine) sugar**, extra

raspberries, to serve

icing (confectioners') sugar, for dusting

Preheat the oven to 160°C (315°F/Gas 2–3). Grease ten 125 ml (4 fl oz/1/2 cup) ramekins or ovenproof moulds with butter and dust the inside of each with sugar.

Put the cream and milk in a saucepan over low heat and bring almost to the boil. Add the chocolate and stir over low heat until the chocolate has melted and is well combined. Stir in the orange zest.

Whisk the eggs and sugar in a large bowl for 5 minutes, or until pale and thick. Whisk a little of the hot chocolate cream into the eggs, then pour the egg mixture onto the remaining chocolate cream, whisking continuously.

Divide the mixture among the ramekins. Put the custards in a large roasting tin and pour in enough hot water to come halfway up the sides of the ramekins. Cover the tin with foil and bake for 30–35 minutes, or until the custards are set. Immediately remove the ramekins from the water bath. Set aside to cool completely. Turn out onto a serving dish, top with the raspberries and dust with icing sugar.

on the side

custard sauces

Eggs, sugar and milk: the foundation for these sublime, silky-smooth custards. Pour over baked puddings, warm tarts or fruit pies.

crème anglaise

Whisk 4 egg yolks and 115 g (4 oz/1/2 cup) caster (superfine) sugar in a bowl until thick and pale. Combine 200 ml (7 fl oz) milk and 200 ml (7 fl oz) pouring cream in a saucepan. Split 1 vanilla bean in half, scrape out the seeds and add the bean and seeds to the saucepan (alternatively, if you don't have a vanilla bean, substitute 1 teaspoon natural vanilla extract). Slowly bring almost to the boil. Strain the milk mixture onto the egg yolk mixture, stirring to combine. Discard the vanilla bean. Return the mixture to a clean saucepan, then cook over medium–low heat, stirring constantly with a wooden spoon until the mixture is thick enough to coat the back of the spoon. Do not allow the mixture to boil or the custard will curdle. Serve the custard hot, warm or chilled. If serving chilled, lay plastic wrap directly on the surface of the custard to prevent a skin forming and refrigerate for up to 2 days. Serve with desserts such as Pear tart tatin, Apple and cherry crostade and Spiced quince charlotte. Makes about 500 ml (17 fl oz/2 cups).

orange custard

Make one quantity of crème anglaise using 170 g (6 oz/3/4 cup) caster (superfine) sugar. Add 1 tablespoon finely grated orange zest to the milk mixture. Strain the milk mixture onto the egg yolk mixture, and continue to cook the custard, as above. Stir 80 ml (21/2 fl oz/1/3 cup) orange-flavoured liqueur into the cooled custard. Serve with slices such as Rhubarb slice or desserts such as Prune clafoutis. Makes about 580 ml (201/4 fl oz/21/3 cups).

espresso custard

Make one quantity of crème anglaise, as above. Add 25 g (1 oz/1/3 cup) whole coffee beans to the milk mixture, then strain through a sieve after the custard has thickened. Stir 21/2 tablespoons coffee-flavoured liqueur into the cooled custard, if desired. Serve with Mocha self-saucing pudding and cakes such as Flourless chocolate cake. Makes about 500 ml (17 fl oz/2 cups).

creamy sauces

Rich, creamy sauces flavoured with raspberries, honey or caramel — serve with cakes and puddings, or dollop over a bowl of poached or fresh fruit.

raspberry cassis cream

Whip 250 ml (9 fl oz/1 cup) whipping cream in a bowl just until soft peaks form. Combine 125 g (4½ oz/1 cup) fresh raspberries, 1 tablespoon caster (superfine) sugar and 2 tablespoons Cassis in a saucepan, cover, then cook over low heat for 2 minutes, or until the raspberries start to soften and the sugar has dissolved. Remove from the heat and cool. Fold the raspberry mixture into the cream and serve immediately. Serve with Peach galettes or Mixed berry sponge puddings. Makes 500 ml (17 fl oz/2 cups).

rosewater and honey cream

Put 250 ml (9 fl oz/1 cup) whipping cream, 1 tablespoon honey and 3 teaspoons rosewater in a bowl, then whip just until soft peaks form. Serve immediately, scattered with a few rose petals. Serve with Pistachio friands, Semolina syrup slice, Coconut baklava or desserts such as Semolina pudding with saffron apricots. Makes 375 ml (13 fl oz/1½ cups).

coffee caramel cream

Combine 250 ml (9 fl oz/1 cup) whipping cream, 80 g (2¾ oz/⅓ cup) soft brown sugar and 2 tablespoons Kahlua or cold, strong coffee in a bowl. Whip just until soft peaks form. Serve with cakes such as Sunken chocolate dessert cakes or Marble cake. Makes 250 ml (9 fl oz/1 cup).

chocolate sauces

Sinfully rich and totally irresistible, these chocolate sauces can be spooned over baked fruit, cakes, puddings and ice creams. Chocolate plays the starring role here, so use a good-quality chocolate.

dark chocolate sauce

Put 110 g (3³/4 oz/³/4 cup) chopped dark chocolate and 60 g (2¹/4 oz) diced, unsalted butter in a small heatproof bowl. Sit the bowl over a small saucepan of simmering water, stirring frequently until the chocolate and butter have melted and the mixture is smooth. Take care that the base of the bowl doesn't touch the water. Remove from the heat and continue to stir occasionally until the sauce is cool and glossy. Serve warm, as the sauce will continue to thicken as it cools. Serve with Ginger cakes with chocolate centres or White chocolate, almond and cranberry torte. Makes 170 ml (5¹/2 fl oz/²/3 cup).

chocolate fudge sauce

Combine 150 g (5¹/2 oz/1 cup) chopped dark chocolate, 30 g (1 oz) unsalted butter, 2 tablespoons golden syrup (or dark corn syrup) and 150 ml (5 fl oz) pouring cream in a saucepan. Heat gently until the chocolate has melted and the mixture is smooth. Continue to heat, stirring, until the mixture almost reaches boiling point, then remove from the heat and cool a little. Serve warm. Serve with Marble cake, or pour over ice cream. Makes 300 ml (10¹/2 fl oz).

milk chocolate and frangelico sauce

Put 100 g (3¹/2 oz/²/3 cup) chopped milk chocolate and 60 ml (2 fl oz/¹/4 cup) thick (double/heavy) cream in a small heatproof bowl. Sit the bowl over a small saucepan of simmering water, stirring frequently until the chocolate and cream have melted and the mixture is smooth. Take care that the base of the bowl doesn't touch the water. Remove from the heat, stir in 2 tablespoons Frangelico, then continue to stir occasionally until the sauce is cool. Serve warm. Serve with Fig shortcake. Makes 185 ml (6 fl oz/³/4 cup).

tip Frangelico is a hazelnut-flavoured liqueur; substitute Amaretto (bitter almond liqueur), if preferred.

fruity sauces

Vividly coloured, fresh, fruity sauces can be made with just about any fruit in season. Drizzle them over ice cream or yoghurt, or serve with chocolate or sponge cakes.

mango citrus sauce

Combine 300 g (10$1/2$ oz) chopped mango flesh (you will need 1 medium mango for this), 80 ml (2$1/2$ fl oz/$1/3$ cup) freshly squeezed orange juice and the juice of 1 lime in a food processor. Process until the mixture is smooth. Sweeten to taste with 1–2 tablespoons icing (confectioners') sugar, if needed. Serve with cakes such as Sponge cake with strawberries and cream and Lemon honey ricotta cakes. Makes 325 ml (11 fl oz).

spiced blueberry sauce

Combine 300 g (10$1/2$ oz/2 cups) fresh or frozen blueberries, 55 g (2 oz/$1/4$ cup) caster (superfine) sugar, 1 cinnamon stick, 2 strips orange zest, 1 strip lemon zest and 1 teaspoon lemon juice with 2 tablespoons water in a saucepan over low heat. Cover and cook, stirring, for 2–3 minutes, or until the sugar has dissolved. Bring the mixture to a simmer and cook for 5 minutes, or until the blueberries are soft and the sauce has thickened slightly. Remove the cinnamon stick and zest. Cool a little before serving. Serve with Blueberry semolina cakes and Vanilla cream cheese cakes. Makes 250 ml (9 fl oz/1 cup).

passionfruit and palm sugar sauce

Combine 60 g (2$1/4$ oz/$1/3$ cup) chopped palm sugar (or soft brown sugar) and 150 ml (5 fl oz) water in a saucepan. Cook over low heat for 5 minutes, or until the sugar has dissolved. Add 170 ml (5$1/2$ fl oz/$2/3$ cup) passionfruit pulp (you will need about 8 large passionfruit), bring to a simmer and cook for 10–15 minutes, or until reduced and thickened slightly. Strain the mixture, pressing firmly on the pulp to extract all the juice. Return 1 tablespoon of the seeds back to the sauce, stir to combine well, then cool. Serve with Baked passionfruit cheesecake. Makes 125 ml (4 fl oz/$1/2$ cup).

boozy sauces

Dress up puddings and cakes with these adults-only sauces. Serve them warm or at room temperature.

rum and raisin caramel sauce

Combine 2½ tablespoons raisins, chopped, and 80 ml (2½ fl oz/⅓ cup) rum in a small bowl, cover with plastic wrap and leave to stand for 2 hours. Put 230 g (8 oz/ 1 cup) caster (superfine) sugar and 125 ml (4 fl oz/½ cup) water in a small saucepan, stirring to dissolve the sugar. Then, without stirring, bring slowly to a boil. Cook the mixture over medium heat for 12–13 minutes, or until the liquid turns a deep caramel colour. Working quickly, remove the caramel from the heat, add the raisin mixture and 125 ml (4 fl oz/½ cup) cream, taking care as the caramel is very hot and the mixture will spit. Swirl the pan to combine well, stirring a little if needed, then cool slightly. Stir in 1 teaspoon natural vanilla extract. Serve the sauce warm or at room temperature. Serve with Pear dumplings. Makes 375 ml (13 fl oz/1½ cups).

apple, clove and brandy sauce

Combine 650 g (1 lb 7 oz) peeled, cored and chopped granny smith apples (about 3 apples), 55 g (2 oz/¼ cup) caster (superfine) sugar and 125 ml (4 fl oz/½ cup) apple juice in a saucepan. Cover, then bring to a simmer and cook the apples over medium heat for 10 minutes, or until very soft. Add 1 tablespoon softened unsalted butter, a large pinch of ground cloves and 60 ml (2 fl oz/¼ cup) brandy and, using a food processor or blender, purée the mixture until smooth. Serve warm or at room temperature. Serve with cakes such as Orange and prune rice cake or Olive oil and sweet wine cake. Makes about 625 ml (21½ fl oz/2½ cups).

marmalade-whisky sauce

Combine 210 g (7½ oz/⅔ cup) sweet orange marmalade, 2 tablespoons lemon juice and ½ teaspoon ground cinnamon (optional) in a small saucepan. Bring to a simmer, then cover and cook over low–medium heat, stirring often, for 5 minutes, or until the marmalade has melted and the mixture is smooth. Remove from the heat and stir in 80 ml (2½ fl oz/⅓ cup) whisky, then leave to stand until cooled and slightly thickened. Serve warm. Serve with Cream cheese soufflés, or with cakes such as Guinness spice cake or Lemon and honey ricotta cake. Makes about 250 ml (9 fl oz/1 cup).

index

Published by Murdoch Books Pty Limited

Murdoch Books Australia
Pier 8/9, 23 Hickson Road, Millers Point NSW 2000
Phone: +61 (0)2 8220 2000 Fax: +61 (0)2 8220 2558

Murdoch Books UK Limited
Erico House, 6th Floor North, 93–99 Upper Richmond Road
Putney, London SW15 2TG
Phone: + 44 (0) 20 8785 5995 Fax: + 44 (0) 20 8785 5985

Chief Executive: Juliet Rogers
Publisher: Kay Scarlett

Concept and art direction: Vivien Valk
Project manager: Janine Flew
Photographer: Ian Hofstetter
Stylist: Jane Collins
Food preparation: Joanne Kelly
Editor: Kim Rowney
Food editor: Leanne Kitchen
Additional text: Louise Pickford
Designer: Lauren Camilleri
Recipes by: Vanessa Broadfoot, Fiona Hammond, Leanne Kitchen,
Kathy Knudsen, Louise Pickford, Rebecca Truda
Production: Monika Paratore

National Library of Australia Cataloguing-in-Publication Data: Bake it. Includes index.
ISBN 1 74045 467 7. 1. Baked products.
(Series: It series (Sydney, N.S.W.)). 641.815

Printed by Sing Cheong Printing Co. Ltd. in 2005. PRINTED IN HONG KONG.
Reprinted 2006.

IMPORTANT: Those who might be at risk from the effects of salmonella poisoning (the elderly,
pregnant women, young children and those suffering from immune deficiency diseases) should
consult their doctor with any concerns about eating raw eggs.

The publisher would like to thank MUD Australia and Bison Homewares for their assistance in the
photography for this book.